GENESIS

WESLEY BIBLE STUDIES

wesleyan
PUBLISHING HOUSE
wphstore.com

CONTENTS

INTRODUCTION

A Real Page-Turner

Do you enjoy reading a book that keeps you turning the pages? Perhaps an intriguing suspense novel grabs your interest and won't let go. Maybe it's a fascinating historical novel or a revealing biography that glues your eyes to every page you turn. Or does a nature study exert a magnetic pull on your attention? Whether suspense, history, biography, or nature fits your style, you will find it in this study of Genesis. Indeed, you will find all of these subjects and more in this study.

A PERFECT CREATION

Everything began with God. He simply spoke, and the heavens and the earth came into existence. Space, matter, and time exist by His creative power. Without His design and command, there would be nothing. Think about that the next time you look at a sunrise or see a hawk soar or a fish leap or a dog run or a flower bloom or a fruit tree blossom. And think about this: God created everything for humans' comfort and enjoyment before He created the first man and woman and placed them in the garden of Eden—a paradise.

A MARRED CREATION

Unfortunately, our first parents succumbed to temptation and fell into sin. As a result, they lost their fellowship with God and incurred a death penalty, eviction from Eden, and a future filled with pain and suffering. God placed a curse on all creation, and only His grace and mercy stood in stark contrast to the darkness of sin.

AN ALL-ENCOMPASSING FLOOD

As the human race expanded, so did evil. Sinning became so rampant that God destroyed the earth with a flood. Only Noah, who found grace in the eyes of the Lord, and his family survived. God had instructed Noah to build an ark according to His specifications. Noah obeyed, although it had never rained on the earth, and as he built he preached to his ungodly contemporaries. Finally, Noah, his wife, and their children entered the ark, and God shut them in. And then the flood came and destroyed everyone and everything outside the ark.

However, the human race that emerged after the flood defied God at Babel. God responded to this insolence by choosing one man, Abram, through whom He would build a chosen people and bless the entire world.

ONE MAN'S FAMILY

Abram was not perfect. Nor were his descendants. But Abram answered God's call and faithfully served Him with few exceptions. By faith he believed God would give him a son—although the prospect was humanly impossible—and he saw God keep His promise.

Genesis continues telling its story through the lives of Isaac, Jacob, and Joseph. Each of these prominent descendants of Abram (Abraham) experienced God's faithfulness in spite of their flaws.

The Genesis story ends with a heartwarming story of family reconciliation and forgiveness.

Expect to see your story and God's goodness in Genesis. Let each study also warm your heart to God's love and faithfulness. And may your eyes see Him displaying His wisdom and power in your life. Study diligently, prayerfully, and devotionally.

1

CREATION PRAISES GOD'S GOODNESS

Genesis 1:1–4, 26–31; 2:7–9, 16–17

God's creation reflects His nature and character.

Step outside on a clear night, gaze into the heavens, marvel at the number of twinkling stars, and ponder the greatness and wisdom of God, the Creator. Consider the complexity of the human body or the migratory patterns of birds or the beautiful composition of a rose, and be amazed at the Creator's infinite intelligence. Pluck a ripe tomato or an ear of corn or pick a peach and consider the Creator's love and goodness in providing such items and more for food.

This study reveals our Creator's character, power, wisdom, and goodness, and fills our souls with awe and gratitude.

COMMENTARY

Where did life come from? What is our purpose? What kind of world is this? What kind of maker made it? Is there more reason for despair or for hope? These are universal questions, and Genesis 1–2 gives us food for thought and action as we seek the meaning of life's origins, purposes, and destiny.

Ancient humans had these fundamental questions as well. All cultures have stories about how the world came into being and what its future may be. There are numerous accounts in the various cultural traditions that speak of wars and sex among the gods, of capricious tricks and deceit by the heavenly beings, and general heavenly chaos as how the world and humans came to be.

Genesis 1–3 and other Old Testament passages present a very different picture of our origins and purposes and, more particularly, of the single Creator of the world. There is a message in this passage that gives meaning and hope to human hearts. There is an author of life, and the author can be known by virtue of His works, as well as His personal revelation in history.

In the Beginning God Created the Heavens and the Earth (Gen. 1:1–4)

Elohim, the early plural and generic name for God shared with other Mesopotamian cultures, is the source of both the earth and the heavens that cover the earth. Interestingly, the verb *created* (*bara*) is singular, suggesting that the plural name operates with singular purpose in creating the heavens and the earth. God is the only subject of this verb in the Hebrew Scriptures, and the word carries the idea of God bringing to reality that which had never existed before, whether it refers to whales, His image in humans, "new heavens and new earth" in Isaiah 65:17, or the new heart David sought in Psalm 51:10. The afflicted author of Psalm 102:25 and the writer of Isaiah 40:21 also made reference to the truth of this first verse: God can create out of nothing.

Now the earth was formless and empty, darkness was over the surface of the deep (Gen. 1:2). Like a body without breath, the earth was without life and waiting for its animation. How long it may have been in this condition is not told. But there was hope for life because **the Spirit of God was hovering over the waters** (v. 2). Ancient people feared the deep waters of the sea; they wondered what lay below. And when we wonder what may be below, it is good to remember the Spirit of God is still present over the deep waters.

And God said, "Let there be light" (v. 3). God is the source of light throughout both testaments. Light is necessary for life itself as well as our ability to see the rest of creation. In 2 Samuel 22:29, David declared, "The LORD turns my darkness into light."

WORDS FROM WESLEY

Genesis 1:1

Observe 1. The effect produced, *The heaven and the earth*—
That is, the world, including the whole frame and furniture of the
universe. But 'tis only the visible part of the creation that Moses
designs to give an account of. Yet even in this there are secrets
which cannot be fathomed, nor accounted for. But from what we
see of heaven and earth, we may infer the eternal power and godhead of the great Creator. . . .

Observe 2. The author and cause of this great work, God. The
Hebrew word is *Elohim*; which (1) seems to mean the Covenant
God, being derived from a word that signifies to swear. (2) The plu-
rality of persons in the Godhead, Father, Son, and Holy Ghost. The
plural name of God in Hebrew, which speaks of him as many . . . is
to us a favour of life unto life, confirming our faith in the doctrine
of the Trinity, which, tho' but darkly intimated in the Old Testament,
is clearly revealed in the New.

Observe 3. The manner how this work was effected; God created,
that is, made it out of nothing. There was not any preexistent matter
out of which the world was produced. The fish and fowl were indeed
produced out of the waters, and the beasts and man out of the earth;
but that earth and those waters were made out of nothing.

Observe 4. When this work was produced; *In the beginning*—
That is, in the beginning of time. Time began with the production of
those beings that are measured by time. Before the beginning of time
there was none but that Infinite Being that inhabits eternity. Should
we ask why God made the world no sooner, we should but darken
counsel by words without knowledge; for how could there be sooner
or later in eternity? (ENOT)

Even before the first person needed light, God knew our need
for light in order that life might flourish and that we might see that
flourishing. In the Hebrews' understanding, the day begins with
darkness or sunset and is followed in the latter part of the "day" by
sunrise. Hence their understanding of a day being evening and
morning reflects the pattern of creation that is followed in this passage. Every day God brings light out of darkness. **God saw that
the light was good, and he separated the light from the darkness**

(Gen. 1:4). Paul also used this metaphor in describing the change in Christians: "For God, who said, 'Let light shine out of darkness,' made his light shine in our hearts to give us the light of the knowledge of the glory of God in the face of Christ" (2 Cor. 4:6). Salvation itself is a creation of light out of darkness.

Then God Said, Let Us Make Man in Our Image and in Our Likeness (Gen. 1:26–27)

Skipping over the rest of the days of creation, our study comes to the second part of the sixth day's creation. Although many assume that only humans were created on day six, land animals were as well. God used the plural of majesty: **Let us** (as He also did in Gen. 11:7 and other Old Testament passages to speak of the court of heaven) **make man in our image, in our likeness, and let them rule** (1:26). Humans were to be the stewards of His creation who would have dominion over the rest of created life. God shaped the earth on the first three days of creation and populated the earth with life on days four through six. Then He designated to humans the authority to be stewards or managers of His creation. One way humans are responsible to God is through this management responsibility.

In verse 27, we encounter three occurrences of the word *bara*. **So God created man in his own image, in the image of God he created him; male and female he created them**. Genesis has already told its readers of God and creation, so what is added here is **in his own image**, that is, God's. Many books have been written about this concept. Notice that the text does not say the image is in humans, but rather that humans are in the image. This wording is important, because much is written about what is in the constitution of human beings that is the image of God. When one says the image is in us, scholars and others try to figure out what part of us is the image. Is it brains, color of skin, gender, mental ability, or capacity for relationship? When answering this question becomes the focus, we realize some people may have more or less of what-ever is considered ideal. This realization then becomes a means of discrimination and oppression as demonstrated in slavery, poor treatment of mentally handicapped persons and prisoners of war, and oppression of believers in other religions over the years. The text simply asserts that humans—both male and female—are the image of God. In 1:26, the text also mentions **likeness**, which some scholars distinguish from **image**. Most likely, however, the two words represent the same concept. If this view is correct, then James 3:9 supports this nondiscriminatory point of view: "With the tongue we praise our Lord and Father, and with it we curse men, who have been made in God's likeness."

WORDS FROM WESLEY

Genesis 1:26

"And God," the three-one God, "said, Let us make man in our image, after our likeness. So God created man in His own image, in the image of God created he him" (Gen. 1:26, 27)—Not barely in His natural image, a picture of His own immortality; a spiritual being, endued with understanding, freedom of will, and various affections—nor merely in His political image, the governor of this lower world, having "dominion over the fishes of the sea, and over all the earth"—but chiefly in His moral image; which, according to the apostle, is "righteousness and true holiness" (Eph. 4:24). In this image of God was man made. "God is love": Accordingly, man at his creation was full of love; which was the sole principle of all his tempers, thoughts, words, and actions. God is full of justice, mercy, and truth; so was man as he came from the hands of his Creator. God is spotless purity; and so man was in the beginning pure from every sinful blot; otherwise God could not have pronounced him, as well as all the other work of His hands, "very good" (Gen. 1:31). This he could not have been, had he not been pure from sin, and filled with righteousness and true holiness. For there is no medium: If we suppose an intelligent creature not to love God, not to be right-eous and holy, we necessarily suppose him not to be good at all; much less to be "very good." (WJW, vol. 6, 66–67)

God Blessed Them and Said to Them (Gen. 1:28–30)

The One who created everything then gave the creation His blessing. God is not just the author of life; He is also the one who blesses life with His words. He is not only above His creation; He exists in relation to it, as later His Word in Christ would more fully demonstrate. **Be fruitful and increase in number; fill the earth and subdue it** (v. 28). Much like the stewardship parables in the Gospels, God gave assignments that He expects those made in His image to fulfill. **Rule over the fish of the sea and the birds of the air and over every living creature that moves on the ground** (v. 28).

Part of the blessing of God is the place of human responsibility in carrying out the management of this great worldwide park of which we are the rangers, charged with looking after the land and life God has made.

Then God said, "I give you every seed-bearing plant . . . for food" (v. 29). Did this original command indicate that before the fall of Adam and Eve humans were to be vegetarian? Did animal diet and sacrifice for humans only become an option after the fall? Possibly, but we cannot be certain. **And to . . . everything that has the breath of life in it — I give every green plant for food** (v. 30). Again, there is no indication of a carnivorous diet. **And it was so.** Of course, God had made it so.

All That God Made Was Good (Gen. 1:31)

From the point of view of God, the creation was "good, good," which is the way the Hebrew language says that it was the best possible outcome. God was pleased that everything had gone according to His spoken commands.

The story that begins in Genesis 1 continues through 2:3. Chapter and verse divisions were added much later — sometimes not so appropriately. This first account is the broad, universal view. The second account is more of a local view. Instead of just using *elohim* as the name for the Creator, the text adds *YHWH* (*Yahweh*). Instead of a cosmic view, it moves to Eden. Instead of waters in general, it identifies specific rivers. Instead of man and woman, it is Adam into whom God breathes life, and Eve, who is from Adam. The view is much more personal and indicative of the covenant between God and humanity.

WORDS FROM WESLEY

Genesis 2:7

To express the creation of this new thing, he takes a new word: a word (some think) borrowed from the potter's forming his vessel upon the wheel. The body of man is curiously wrought. And the soul takes its rise from the breath of heaven. It came immediately from God; He gave it to be put into the body (Eccl. 12:7) as afterwards He gave the tables of stone of His own writing to be put into the ark. 'Tis by it that man is a living soul, that is, a living man. The body would be a worthless, useless carcase, if the soul did not animate it. (ENOT)

The Lord God Formed Adam and Gave Him the Breath of Life (Gen. 2:7)

The Hebrew word for "dust" is *adamah*, from which the name Adam derives. Man is literally dust, and this dust has no life without God's breath (*ruach*) being given to it. *Ruach* is also the Hebrew word for "breath," "spirit," and "wind." The story of the creation of the first human makes perfect sense if one looks backward. Today, a living, breathing person may walk around and do all the things people do. But eventually every person dies, and as nature follows its course, the body decomposes into dust. One of the primary differences between a living, breathing person and the eventual remains of the body is that the living person has breath or spirit, while the person who has passed on does not. Thus, by deduction, you might think that breath or spirit animated that which is now dust or *adamah*. God is the Spirit who gives us breath. Human life is formed and animated by God.

A Garden in Eden (Gen. 2:8–9)

God prepared a place for humans to flourish—a lovely garden of delight or pleasure, which is what *Eden* means. We do not know the location of this garden, but most scholars believe it may have been in the Mesopotamian river valley formed by the Tigris and Euphrates rivers near the Persian Gulf. The main point of emphasis is that God had prepared a place for humankind to flourish. There were trees that were aesthetically pleasing to the eye, and there were trees there that were nourishing with good fruit. A similar scene takes place in Revelation 22:1–5, where the final blessedness of God's people is described. **In the middle of the garden were the tree of life and the tree of the knowledge of good and evil** (Gen. 2:9). The Tree of Life was allowed for food and had eternal life for humans who could eat of it and live forever.

God Gives a Command and Free Will to Humans (Gen. 2:16–17)

And the LORD God commanded the man, "You are free to eat from any tree in the garden; but you must not eat from the tree of the knowledge of good and evil, for when you eat of it you will surely die" (vv. 16–17).

God's command assumed that Adam and Eve had the power of choice. They had tremendous freedom to eat from any of the trees that were good for food, but there were limits to this freedom. Without choices, freedom would be meaningless, and human beings would be automatons. Adam and Eve, as the original representatives of all humanity, chose wrongly, just as sometimes our representatives in federal government choose wrongly and the consequences fall on all of us whom they represent. This concept of federal headship is true to life. There are some choices that lead to death not only for ourselves but for those we represent.

WORDS FROM WESLEY

Genesis 2:16–17

God forbade man to eat of this tree, in token of His sovereign authority, and for the exercise of man's love, and the trial of his obedience. The words added, "In the day thou eatest thereof thou shalt surely die," or literally, "In dying thou shalt die," mean, not only, "Thou shalt certainly die" but, "Thou shalt suffer every kind of death": Thy soul as well as thy body shall die. And, indeed, if God made man upright or holy; if man at first enjoyed the life of God, including holiness joined with blessedness; and if the miserable state of the soul (as well as the dissolution of the body) is in the Scripture termed "death"; it plainly follows, that the original threatening includes nothing less than a loss of man's original uprightness, of his title to God's favour, and happy life of communion with God. (WJW, vol. 9, 402)

DISCUSSION

Discuss how the diverse and amazing forms of life you see in nature came into existence.

1. Why do you think Genesis 1:1 uses a plural form of God's name?

2. Read Genesis 1:3. What purpose do you believe was served by God's creating light before He created anything else?

3. How does natural light enhance the quality of human life? How does spiritual light enhance your life?

4. Read Genesis 1:16 and 27. How do these verses support the pro-life position? How do they oppose the notion that women are second-class citizens?

5. Do you agree or disagree that Christians should observe one day a week as a day of worship and rest?

6. Read Genesis 2:7. What distinguishes human beings from animals? How would you respond to the claim that man is a human animal?

7. Did work originate because of sin? Explain your answer.

8. What wrong applications of free will have you observed or read about lately? How will you employ the gift of free will to make right choices?

PRAYER

Heavenly Father, thank You for being our creator, for revealing yourself through the glory of the universe.

2

KEEPING OUR VISION SHARP

Genesis 3:1, 6–7, 15–17, 20–24

Sin distorts our spiritual vision, but God's grace can restore our sight.

An insightful old preacher observed, "I used to say civilization was going to the dogs. I no longer say that out of respect for dogs."

Although the observation is humorous, it is also sad. We grieve when we read or hear about injustice, atrocities, thievery, cheating, lying, fighting, bickering, and so many other sins that are common to human life. We recognize that the whole world languishes in sin, and even believers are not immune to temptation. How do we account for the presence and vitality of sin? This study supplies the answer, and we may be surprised to learn that sin began in a paradise.

COMMENTARY

In the space of two chapters, the author of Genesis quickly moved from nothing but God to a universe of light, life, and love. The cosmos appeared, and two people were living in Eden—the garden of delight. Out of the *adamah*, or dust of the earth, God had made *adam*, a human, in fact, *the* human; and out of the first human, God had made a second one because it was not good for the first person to be alone. Over what may well have been a long span of time, the author sped to the critical event that was key to the whole story of humanity's need for redemption. This redemption was first forecast in the words the Lord God spoke to the serpent: "And I will put enmity between you and the woman, and between your offspring and hers; he will crush your

head, and you will strike his heel" (Gen. 3:15). These words set
the stage for the ebb and flow of the history of God's work in
the Old Testament. This flow will include the necessity of priests,
the visions of prophets, and the longings of poets. This passage
anticipates ultimate victory in the work of the Messiah's first
coming that has already occurred and His second coming that is
yet to occur.

A Crafty Serpent (Gen. 3:1)

The serpent was one of God's creatures, included in the
phrase "and God saw that it was good" in Genesis 1. The serpent
is not identified as the Devil or Satan in the passage, but apparently the spirit of evil entered this snake in order to tempt the
woman. **He said to the woman, "Did God really say, 'You
must not eat from any tree in the garden'?"** (3:1). Compare
this with what the Lord God actually said to Adam in 2:16–17.
God had not said this; in fact, all the food-producing trees in the
garden, including the Tree of Life, were available for Adam and
the woman. All the available goodness of the garden seemed to
pale in comparison to the tree that was off-limits. The woman
also added an additional prohibition to what God said when she
stated that God said not to touch the tree.

WORDS FROM WESLEY
Genesis 3:1

The tempter, the Devil in the shape of a serpent. Multitudes of
them fell; but this that attacked our first parents, was surely the prince
of the devils. Whether it was only the appearance of a serpent, or a
real serpent, acted and possessed by the Devil, is not certain. The
Devil chose to act his part in a serpent, because it is subtile creature.
It is not improbable, that reason and speech were then the known
properties of the serpent. And therefore Eve was not surprised at his
reasoning and speaking, which otherwise she must have been. (ENOT)

Succumbing to Temptation (Gen. 3:6–7)

Leading up to these verses, the serpent suggested to the woman that God had lied about death as the penalty for her disobedience, and he also suggested she would become like God, with knowledge of good and evil. Was a promotion in status in the works for the woman so that *Yahweh Elohim* might not be necessary anymore? Could she become morally and spiritually autonomous? Then she would know not only good, but also evil, and she would decide what was wrong and what was right all by herself.

Note the progress of temptation in this passage. It is **good for food** (physically inviting), **pleasing to the eye** (aesthetically seductive), and **desirable for gaining wisdom** (intellectually attractive) (v. 6). Compare this with 1 John 2:16 and Luke 4:3–9. Rationalizing God's command in order to do what one wishes is as old as Eden.

WORDS FROM WESLEY

Genesis 3:6

Is it not natural to us, to care for the body, at the expense of the soul? This was one ingredient in the sin of our first parents (Gen. 3:6). O how happy might we be, if we were but at half the pains about our souls, which we bestow upon our bodies! If that question, "What must I do to be saved?" did but run near so often through our minds, as those, "What shall we eat? What shall we drink? Wherewithal shall we be clothed?" (WJW, vol. 9, 442)

Having considered what was to be gained but not what was to be lost, the woman took fruit and ate it and also gave some to Adam so he could taste it as well. Adam made no resistance to the woman's offer of her newfound pleasure—not even a word about God's command.

Then the eyes of both of them were opened, and they realized they were naked (Gen. 3:7). The state of dreamlike innocence was forfeited. Immediately Adam and the woman realized they were naked and vulnerable, and they fashioned for themselves some protection in the form of fig leaves. They were also afraid of God because they had rejected His authority and protection. One may read their rationalizations in Genesis 3:8–13.

Then came the fallout for the disobedience; the curse fell on the participants in the same order as the process of their disobedience. First, the curse fell on the serpent, then on the woman, and finally on Adam. The focus of this study is on the curse upon the woman and then Adam.

The Effects of the Curse (Gen. 3:15–17)

And I will put enmity between you and the woman, and between your offspring and hers; he will crush your head, and you will strike his heel (v. 15). Venomous snakes are scary to most everyone. There could be no better personification of evil than snakes! Later, in Numbers 21:4–9, God provided a prefiguring of the cure for human rebellion when, in response to the disobedience of the people, snakes invaded the camp and some Hebrews died from the venom. God told Moses to make a bronze snake on a pole so that people could look to that sign and be cured of the bite. Jesus reminded Nicodemus of this sign in John 3:14 and seems to have implied that this Old Testament event prefigured His own death on the cross. It was at the cross that the serpent struck the heel of the Messiah but the Messiah crushed the head of the serpent. Later, in Acts 28:3–6, Paul shook off the attack of a viper, and people thought perhaps he was a god because he survived the attack. Snakes are no match for God's authority!

It is worth pointing out that **with pain you will give birth to children** (Gen. 3:16) was made well before the days of anesthesia and epidurals, which may ease but not eliminate the pain or "discomfort" (as some instructors call it). There is good reason that *labor* is the word commonly used for the process of birthing a child. It is difficult work, and these words were actually a prophecy of something that had not yet happened, if looked at historically. Cain, Abel, and Seth had not yet been born, but when these sons came along, pain came for the woman, both in the birth itself and later in the first fratricide committed by Cain against Abel. In this curse was also an affirmation that the human race would continue. Children would come. God was not done with Adam and the woman. Later Seth would continue the line of Adam, leading to the birth of the Messiah. **Your desire will be for your husband, and he will rule over you** (v. 16). Parts A and B of this verse are parallel ways of making the same point, but part C is another aspect of the curse brought on by the woman's disobedience. The creative intention of the Lord God in bringing the woman out of Adam was that they be one flesh, not only in reference to sexual intercourse, but also in equality of partnership as depicted in the "one flesh" relationship. However, the woman would now be ruled by the man as the curse fell upon her.

WORDS FROM WESLEY

Genesis 3:15

By "the righteousness which is of faith" is meant, that condition of justification (and, in consequence, of present and final salvation, if we endure therein unto the end), which was given by God to fallen man, through the merits and mediation of His only-begotten Son. This was in part revealed to Adam, soon after his fall; being contained in the original promise, made to him and his seed, concerning the Seed of the Woman, who should "bruise the serpent's head" (Gen. 3:15). (WJW, vol. 5, 68)

It is worth remembering that in the New Testament, Paul, a former Jewish rabbi, stated that husbands ought once again to "love their wives as their own bodies," and he further stated, "He who loves his wife loves himself" (Eph. 5:28–29). Such a view suggests that the created pre-fall mutuality is on the way to being restored and that the church community should reflect this "new creation." It is clear that the mutual submission mentioned in Ephesians 5:21 is to counteract the effects of the fall in which first the woman and then Adam asserted themselves, going against God's will for His creation. It is also clear that a woman was in partnership with God in Messiah's birth and that women are to be declarers of the gospel.

This study does not deal with the last two verses of the curse on Adam, but the substance of those verses is included in verse 17. However, instead of trees that were "pleasing to the eye and good for food," Adam would see "thorns and thistles" and "plants of the field." And at death, the first couple would return to the dust, or *adamah*, from which Adam came. Think of the contrast between Eden with its rivers and lush vegetation and the harsh Middle-Eastern aridity and dust.

The Mother of All the Living (Gen. 3:20–24)

Have you noticed that Eve, whose name means "living," has not been called Eve until this point in the narrative? After the fall, Adam named her, indicating his rule over her in the now-fallen world. God originally named her woman (*ishah*) because she was taken out of man (*ish*). **The LORD God made garments of skin for Adam and his wife and clothed them** (v. 21). The Lord God upgraded the fig-leaf clothing they had made for themselves, offering a better covering for their shame. **And the LORD God said, "The man has now become like one of us, knowing good and evil"** (v. 22). Both Adam and Eve are referred to as **the man**, which meant "humanity" and included both male and female. In a strange and eerie way, Satan's prediction became partially true. Previously, Adam and the woman had known only good, but now they also knew evil—and its consequences. **Knowing** in Hebrew means not just an intellectual understanding but a more intimate acquaintance, as in Genesis 4:1 in the King James Version. As to the possibility that humanity would eat from the Tree of Life and live forever, God did not want humanity to live forever in the now-contaminated universe that resulted from their sin. **So the LORD God banished him from the Garden of Eden to work the ground from which he had been taken** (3:23). Man had fallen from the fruitfulness of the garden to toil in the barrenness of the dust from whence he had come, and man would eventually return to dust himself. The word of God breathed by the Spirit is the source and essence of life because only God's word and Spirit can make dust into humans.

WORDS FROM WESLEY

Genesis 3:20

God having named the man, and called him Adam, which signifies red earth, he in farther token of dominion named the woman, and called her Eve—That is, life. Adam bears the name of the dying body, Eve of the living soul. The reason of the name is here given, some think by Moses the historian, others by Adam himself, because she was—That is, was to be the mother of all living. He had called her Isha, woman, before, as a wife; here he calls her Evah, life, as a mother. Now, (1) If this was done by divine direction, it was an instance of God's favour, and, like the new naming of Abraham and Sarah, it was a seal of the covenant, and an assurance to them, that notwithstanding their sin, He had not reversed that blessing wherewith He had blessed them, "Be fruitful and multiply": it was likewise a confirmation of the promise now made, that the seed of the woman, of this woman, should break the serpent's head. (2) If Adam did of himself, it was an instance of his faith in the word of God. (ENOT)

After he drove the man out, he placed on the east side of the Garden of Eden cherubim and a flaming sword flashing back and forth to guard the way to the tree of life (v. 24).

Adam and Eve needed to be protected from endless life in a difficult and harsh existence separated from God's original plan for them. Preventing them from getting to the Tree of Life was a sign of the long-term love of God. A second Adam rescued humans from the inheritance the first man left us. This Adam provides a path back to the garden of delight and to the Tree of Life that reappears in Revelation 22:1–3 to yield its fruit year-round, if years even matter then.

DISCUSSION

Discuss how sin marred God's perfect creation and destroyed the cordial relationship that existed between God and humans.

1. Read Genesis 3:1. Are you ever tempted to question what God has said? What specific occasion do you recall when you felt tempted to question Him?

2. How do you explain the fact that God had created the serpent but the serpent was involved in an evil plot?

3. Read Genesis 3:4. Do you believe God's integrity is questioned today? If so, how?

4. What do you think the Devil uses today to appeal to the lust of the eye?

5. Why do you think Adam accepted the forbidden fruit Eve offered?

6. What part of the curse do you think might have been the hardest for Adam and Eve to experience? Explain.

7. If someone asked you describe an ideal marriage, how would you respond?

8. Read Genesis 3:21. How does this verse picture God's saving grace?

9. Read Genesis 3:21–24. What do you learn from these verses about God's character?

PRAYER

Lord, please forgive us when we repent; keep us restless until we have confessed our sins to You.

YOU CAN'T KEEP GOD FROM LOVING YOU

Genesis 6:9–11; 7:24—8:5; 9:8–11, 16

God relentlessly maintains His covenant relationship with humanity.

In 2012 a wildfire torched a scenic area in the foothills just west of Colorado Springs, Colorado. Known as the Waldon Canyon fire, the raging inferno claimed two lives, destroyed 347 beautiful homes, and scarred the landscape. The following year rain fell on the burned area, cascaded down the barren canyon, washed out a highway, swept away cars, overflowed creeks, ruined some houses and businesses in a nearby town, and carried two people to their deaths. Anyone who has been victimized by a flood can testify to its dreadful force.

This study reviews the most destructive flood in history and explains why it occurred.

COMMENTARY

"In the beginning God created the heavens and the earth" (Gen. 1:1). At the pinnacle of His creative work, God made male and female humans in His image. First, "God formed the man from the dust of the ground and breathed into his nostrils the breath of life" (2:7). "Then the LORD God made a woman from the rib he had taken out of the man" (v. 22). God told Adam and Eve, "You are free to eat from any tree in the garden; but you must not eat from the tree of the knowledge of good and evil, for when you eat of it you will surely die'" (vv. 16–17).

However, a crafty creature lied to Adam and Eve, and they rebelled against God. They ate the forbidden fruit and lost their place in God's presence (Gen. 3). Adam and Eve had many sons and daughters (5:4). Three of their sons are mentioned by name—Cain, Abel, and Seth (4–5). Cain killed Abel, and God cursed him to a life of restless wandering on the earth.

As the human population increased, "the sons of God saw that the daughters of men were beautiful, and they married any of them they chose" (6:2). The identity of these "sons of God" is unclear. Some understand the term as standing for fallen angels, followers of Satan, who mated with human women (see Job 1:6; 2:1). A second explanation is that the "sons of God" were the descendants of Seth and the "daughters of men" were the descendants of Cain; their sin was the intermarriage between the godly and the ungodly. The offspring of Cain were characterized by cleverness, selfishness, sensuality, and ungodliness (Gen. 4:16–24). On the other hand, Seth's offspring were devoted to God (v. 25), consecrated to God (v. 26), enjoyed fellowship with God (5:22), and served God (v. 29). A third position takes "sons of God" to mean the pagan kings. These men were often considered in the ancient Near East to be the children of the gods. According to this interpretation, these kings produced large harems and introduced unprecedented decadence.

Whatever the nature or agents of the sin, it was a symptom of the universal and all-pervasive rebellion of humanity. "Every inclination of the thoughts of his heart was only evil all the time" (6:5). The Lord's "heart was filled with pain" (v. 6) because of this deep and comprehensive rebellion.

"So the LORD said, 'I will wipe mankind, whom I have created, from the face of the earth—men and animals, and creatures that move along the ground, and birds of the air—for I am grieved that I have made them'" (Gen. 6:7). The Hebrew word translated "grieved" can mean "sorry" (NKJV) or "repent" (KJV). This statement is anthropomorphic. God revealed His attitude toward sin in terms of human experience and emotion. While God is unchanging in His holiness and love, He responds freely and appropriately to changes in human behavior. When persons sin or repent of sin, He "changes His mind" in connection with the blessing or punishment appropriate to the situation (Ex. 32:12, 14; 1 Sam. 15:11; 2 Sam. 24:16; Jer. 18:11; Amos 7:3, 6).

God had spared Adam and Eve, as well as all their descendants, until judgment could no longer be avoided. All humanity would die. "But Noah found favor [grace] in the eyes of the LORD" (Gen. 6:8).

Noteworthy Noah (Gen. 6:9–11)

God's "grace" is always His unmerited favor, and Noah's integrity could not earn God's acceptance (Rom. 3:19–20). **Noah was a righteous man** (Gen. 6:9) because his behavior flowed from his relationship with God. He was **blameless among the people of his time** because, unlike them, Noah **walked with God**. In other words, he experienced intimate fellowship with God. This phrase is also used to describe Enoch, who "walked with God; then he was no more, because God took him away" (5:24).

WORDS FROM WESLEY
Genesis 6:9

Noah was a just man—Justified before God by faith in the promised seed; for he was an heir of the righteousness which is by faith (Heb. 11:7). He was sanctified, and had right principles and dispositions implanted in him: and he was righteous in his conversation, one that made conscience of rendering to all their due, to God His due, and to men theirs. And he walked with God as Enoch had done before him: in his generation, even in that corrupt degenerate age. It is easy to be religious when religion is in fashion; but it is an evidence of strong faith to swim against the stream, and to appear for God, when no one else appears for Him: so Noah did, and it is upon record to his immortal honour. (ENOT)

In contrast to Noah, **the earth was corrupt in God's sight** (6:11). The word translated **corrupt** (vv. 11–12) means "to decay and to destroy." The word translated *corrupt* in verse 5 is the same word translated "evil" in reference to the Tree of Knowledge of Good and Evil (2:7). This Hebrew word covers a broad range of words that describe bad events and situations—*adversity, affliction, distress, harm, trouble,* as well as *immorality.* Its root meaning is "to ruin by breaking into pieces." **And** the earth **was full of violence** (v. 11). These verses stand in stark contrast with Genesis 1:3: "God saw all that he had made, and it was very good." In Noah's day, sin's destruction, decay, and brokenness spread to every part of the world. God's creation was ruined and growing worse.

God sent a flood to stop sin in its tracks. He wiped all the corrupted creatures off the face of His planet. He spared Noah and his family as well as enough of each kind of animal to repopulate the earth. In order to save this remnant, He instructed Noah to build an ark. "This is how you are to build it: The ark is to be 450 feet long, 75 feet wide and 45 feet high" (Gen. 6:15). These dimensions indicate the ark was to be shaped like a barge. It would have 33,750 square feet on three decks and over 1.5 million cubic feet. It would be large enough to carry Noah's family and the specified animals. With these proportions, the ark would be about the size of an oil tanker and would survive an ocean voyage.

When Noah received God's directions, he "did everything just as God commanded him" (6:22). His unquestioning obedience to the Lord's directions is mentioned four separate times (6:22; 7:5, 9, 16). There is not even a hint of hesitation. Noah trusted God and obeyed Him. He built the ark and loaded his cargo. He moved his family onboard and "the LORD shut him in" (7:16). Then the rains came down for forty days (v. 17).

The Flood Comes and Goes (Gen. 7:24—8:5)

After all the mountains were covered with the deluge, **the waters flooded the earth for a hundred and fifty days** (v. 24). The destruction was universal and complete. "Every living thing that moved on the earth perished. . . . Everything on dry land that had the breath of life in its nostrils died. Every living thing on the face of the earth was wiped out; men and animals and the creatures that move along the ground and the birds of the air were wiped from the earth" (Gen. 7:21–23).

But God remembered Noah (8:1). In the Bible, when God remembered someone, the Lord acted in his or her best interest out of concern and love. This choice of words points to action based on an earlier promise. God often acted like this in response to the person's prayers (see Gen. 30:22; Ex. 2:24; 1 Sam. 1:19). God not only remembered Noah, but also **all the wild animals and the livestock that were with him in the ark, and he sent a wind over the earth, and the waters receded** (Gen. 8:1).

WORDS FROM WESLEY

Genesis 8:1

And God remembered Noah and every living thing—This is an expression after the manner of men, for not any of his creatures, much less any of his people are forgotten of God. . . . Noah himself, tho' one that had found grace in the eyes of the Lord, yet seemed to be forgotten in the ark; but at length God returned in mercy to him, and that is expressed by His remembering him. (ENOT)

God kept His promise to Noah. He closed **the springs of the deep and the floodgates of the heavens** (v. 2). He stopped the rain and **the water receded steadily from the earth** (v. 3). This process was much slower than the deluge. **At the end of the hundred and fifty days the water had gone down** until, six months after the flood began, **the ark came to rest on the mountains of Ararat** (vv. 3–4). The ark came to rest in a mountain range southeast of the Black Sea and west of the Caspian Sea in what we know today as Turkey. These are some of the highest peaks in the Middle East. However, the floodwaters still covered the lower elevations. So, **the waters continued to recede until the tenth month, and on the first day of the tenth month the tops of the** other **mountains became visible** (8:5).

After Noah, his family, and the animals had spent about a year inside the ark, the earth was completely dry again. "Then God said to Noah, 'Come out of the ark, you and your wife and your sons and their wives. Bring out every kind of living creature that is with you—the birds, the animals, and all the creatures that move along the ground—so they can multiply on the earth and be fruitful and increase in number upon it'" (Gen. 8:15–17). After setting foot on dry ground for good, Noah built an altar and made a sacrifice to the Lord. God received Noah's sacrifice as a "pleasing aroma." The Lord decided never again to destroy the earth by a flood.

The Rainbow Covenant (Gen. 9:8–11, 16)

After repeating His original command to "be fruitful and increase in number and fill the earth" (Gen. 1:28; 9:1), **God said to Noah and to his sons . . . "I now establish my covenant with you and with your descendants after you and with every living creature that was with you"** (vv. 8–9).

A covenant connects two individuals or groups. There were three main types of covenants in the Old Testament era. There was the unconditional royal grant, when a king would give something of great value to a faithful subject for exceptional service. There was the parity covenant between equals, tying them together in mutual respect and/or friendship. Then there was the conditional suzerain-vassal covenant, where a great king claimed the right of absolute sovereignty over a weaker king. He would demand complete loyalty and service. In exchange for the weaker king's faithful service, the great king promised to protect the lesser king and his people. All the covenants involved oaths calling for the death and destruction of either party if he broke his promises.

Therefore, a covenant was the most solemn and binding form of a divine promise. A covenant was a guarantee to a person of the Lord's faithfulness, as well as a God-given reminder of His truthfulness. In the covenants between God and humans in the Bible, God took the initiative. He willingly committed himself before He asked for a pledge.

God said, **I establish my covenant with you** (v. 11). He made the covenant, set the terms and conditions, and promised to stay faithful forever. This agreement was applied to "every living creature" (v. 12). It was unqualified and permanent.

WORDS FROM WESLEY

Genesis 9:11

There shall not any more be a flood—God had drowned the world once, and still it is as provoking as ever; yet He will never drown it any more, for He deals not with us according to our sins. This promise of God keeps the sea and clouds in their decreed place, and sets them gates and bars, Hitherto they shall come (Job 38:10, 11). If the sea should slow but for a few days, as it doth twice every day for a few hours, what desolations would it make? So would the clouds, if such showers as we have sometimes seen, were continued long. But God by flowing seas, and sweeping rains, shews what He could do in wrath; and yet by preserving the earth from being deluged between both, shews what He can do in mercy, and will do in truth. (ENOT)

God's covenant with Noah included a divine promise and human responsibilities. Although humans could eat meat from this point on, they were not to eat blood in the meat (v. 4). God also required that evenhanded human verdicts be issued, especially in the case of murder (v. 6). In addition, God gave humanity the responsibility to repopulate the planet (v. 7). Then He said, **"Never again will all life be cut off by the waters of a flood; never again will there be a flood to destroy the earth"** (v. 11).

"Whenever the rainbow appears in the clouds, I will see it and remember the everlasting covenant between God and all living creatures of every kind on the earth" (v. 16). The rainbow was the sign of God's covenant. Just as a rainbow divided the sky into two parts, God implied He would be split into pieces if He allowed the waters to destroy all living creatures again.

WORDS FROM WESLEY

Genesis 9:16

Nay, as if the eternal Mind needed a memorandum, "I will look upon it that I may remember the everlasting covenant." The rainbow appears when the clouds are most disposed to wet; when we have most reason to fear the rain prevailing, God shews this seal of the promise that it shall not prevail. The rainbow appears when one part of the sky is clear, which imitates mercy remembered in the midst of wrath, and the clouds are hemmed as it were with the rainbow, that it may not overspread the heavens, for the bow is coloured rain, or the edges of a cloud gilded. As God looks upon the bow that He may remember the covenant, so should we, that we also may be ever mindful of the covenant with faith and thankfulness. (ENOT)

DISCUSSION

Discuss your opinion on the view of humanity that asserts that everyone is basically good and capable of making the world a better place.

1. An evolutionist's view of human history might present the human race as constantly improving. How does Genesis 6:9–11 oppose this view?

2. How hard do you think it was for Noah to walk with God when his contemporaries were obviously walking with the Devil?

3. Has your relationship with God made you feel like a member of a minority group? Explain.

4. Read James 4:4–5. Why is it impossible to be a friend of the world and God at the same time?

5. Why do you agree or disagree that the world is becoming increasingly evil?

6. What example of faith did Noah set for you?

7. The Lord shut Noah and his family in the ark (Gen. 7:16). What significance, if any, do you see in this action by the Lord?

8. What do you think of when you see a rainbow?

9. On a scale of one to ten, how secure are God's promises? What divine promise is especially meaningful to you right now?

PRAYER

Lord, keep the influence of the wicked far from us and deliver us from the temptations the world puts in front of us.

4

GOD TAKES THE INITIATIVE

Genesis 12:1–7; 15:1–6

God takes the initiative to call and develop
people who will follow Him.

A rental-truck agency claims that moving is an adventure. It certainly is, and likely the older you are the greater the adventure. A move involves contacting utility providers; packing what may be decades of accumulated stuff; leaving behind familiar surroundings, friends, family members, and numerous memories. At the end of the move, you have to start a new chapter of life, settle into unfamiliar surroundings, find a good church, build new relationships, and learn where to shop. If you have children, the adventure reaches new heights, involving new schools and new friends.

But what if you had to move without knowing your destination? That's what happened to Abram. This study looks at the beginning of his adventure.

COMMENTARY

We can summarize the story of creation found in Genesis 1 with three simple sentences: "In the beginning God created the heavens and the earth" (1:1); "God created man in his own image, in the image of God he created him; male and female he created them" (v. 27); and "God saw all that he had made, and it was very good" (v. 31). However, God's assessment of His creation raises at least two questions: How did the world go bad? Why is there evil in this universe?

In Genesis 2, the author narrowed the focus of the creation narrative in order to set the stage for the answer to these questions.

This account focuses on the first two humans, Adam and Eve, and we can sum it up quickly as well: "God formed the man from the dust of the ground and breathed into his nostrils the breath of life, and the man became a living being" (2:7); "The LORD God took the man and put him in the Garden of Eden to work it and take care of it" (v. 15); "God caused the man to fall into a deep sleep; and while he was sleeping, he took one of the man's ribs . . . made a woman from the rib . . . and he brought her to the man" (vv. 21–22); "God commanded the man, 'You are free to eat from any tree in the garden; but you must not eat from the tree of the knowledge of good and evil, for when you eat of it you will surely die'" (vv. 16–17). How would Adam and Eve respond to God's garden and command?

Genesis 3 answers this question, as well as the issues raised regarding evil in God's good creation. Without any introduction or explanation, a new character entered the garden of Eden. The serpent lied to Adam and Eve. He told them God lied to them about sin. "You will not surely die" when you eat from the Tree of Knowledge of Good and Evil (Gen. 3:4). The serpent lied to them about God and about humans. He told them God wanted to keep them from being like Him and that by eating the fruit they would be God's equal (v. 5).

Adam and Eve believed the serpent and ate the forbidden fruit. Adam and Eve's rebellious act introduced evil, sickness, and death to God's "very good" creation. Nevertheless, God did not abandon His work of love. His grace prevented their immediate death, but He expelled Adam and Eve from His presence (vv. 6–24). The rest of the Bible (Gen. 4 — Rev. 22) tells the story of all God did, does, and will do to bring His people back into His presence. God displayed His answer to our sin in the life of Abraham.

The Lord Acts (Gen. 12:1–3)

With very little introduction or explanation, Genesis 12 opens with God's directive **to Abram, "Leave your country, your people and your father's household and go to the land I will show you"** (v. 1). This call to move required Abram to leave his familiar country, his extended family, and his father's house. God also expected Abram to start traveling and to keep moving until He told him to stop. There is no hint about how the Lord spoke to Abram. Apparently, though, His method of communication with Abram was clear enough that Abram understood the call.

WORDS FROM WESLEY

Genesis 12:1

We have here the call by which Abram was removed out of the land of his nativity into the land of promise, which was designed both to try his faith and obedience, and also to set him apart for God. The circumstances of this call we may be somewhat helped to the knowledge of, from Stephen's speech, Acts 7:2 where we are told, that the God of glory appeared to him to give him this call, appeared in such displays of His glory as left Abram no room to doubt. God spake to him after in divers manners; but this first time, when the correspondence was to be settled, He appeared to him as the God of glory, and spake to him. . . . By this precept he was tried whether he could trust God farther than he saw Him, for he must leave his own country to go to a land that God would shew him; He doth not say, 'tis a land that I will give thee: nor doth He tell him what land it was, or what kind of land; but he must follow God with an implicit faith, and take God's word for it in the general, though he had no particular securities given him, that he should be no loser by leaving his country to follow God. (ENOT)

God's call to sacrifice Abram's comfort was in the present tense: **Leave.** God gave Abram three promises along with His request. All of them were in the future tense. Two focused primarily on Abram and his descendants: **"I will make you into a great**

nation and . . . I will make your name great" (v. 2). God's other promise was to Abram and all humanity: **"I will bless you . . . and you will be a blessing"** (v. 2). The Lord went on to explain this general promise of blessing: **"I will bless those who bless you, and whoever curses you I will curse; and all peoples on earth will be blessed through you"** (v. 3). This promise to bless all peoples on earth found its fulfillment in Jesus Christ, who said, "God so loved the world that he gave his one and only Son, that whoever believes in him shall not perish but have eternal life. For God did not send his Son into the world to condemn the world, but to save the world through him" (John 3:16–17).

God's actions revealed His nature and character. Because the Lord spoke to Abram, we know He is a personal, independent, real being. He is relational. God can communicate with us in ways we understand. He took the initiative in grace and chose to reach out to fallen humanity. In contrast to the serpent, the Lord revealed the truth. He is helpful and sympathetic, seeking to enrich our lives. Because God made promises to Abram without reference to a greater power, He is the supreme authority (Heb. 6:13–18). God's command and promises reveal that He has the wisdom to plan and the power to carry out His plans. Because thousands of years have passed since Adam and Eve rebelled in the garden, we see that God is not limited by time or place. Unlike humans, He is eternal.

Abram's Response (Gen. 12:4–7)

So Abram left, as the LORD had told him; and Lot went with him (v. 4). His obedience to the command implied that Abram had faith in God. The faith that pleases God has three sides. First, it believes in His existence and the truth of His statements. Second, it trusts in God's character and nature. Third, it is loyal to God and obeys Him.

Abram's obedient response to God's call displayed these three aspects of faith. Abram believed in God's existence and the truth of His promises. Abram trusted God's character and he loyally **set out from Haran . . . for the land of Canaan** (vv. 4–5).

Abram traveled through the land as far as the site of the great tree of Moreh at Shechem (v. 6). The town of Shechem would be a major landmark in the life of Abram's grandson Jacob (Gen. 33–34; 37). At this point in Abram's journey, **the LORD** took the initiative again, appeared to Abram, and said, **"To your offspring I will give this land"** (12:7). In response to God's appearance and repeated promise, Abram **built an altar there to the LORD**.

As Abram traveled through the hills of Palestine, a famine forced him to go south to Egypt. Sarai and Abram lied to Pharaoh about their marital status and created a great deal of suffering in the process. The king of Egypt forced Abram and Sarai to take all their belongings out of his country.

Abram and his nephew Lot were both rich men. They owned so much livestock that the land could not support their combined herds. Abram gave Lot first choice of places to settle. Lot took the rich, green valleys near the cities of Sodom and Gomorrah. As a result, Abram went to the hills of Canaan, and they parted ways.

WORDS FROM WESLEY

Genesis 12:7

And the Lord appeared to Abram—Probably in a vision, and spoke to him comfortable words; *Unto thy seed will I give this land*—No place or condition can shut us out from God's gracious visits. Abram is a sojourner, unsettled, among Canaanites, and yet here also he meets with Him that lives, and sees him. Enemies may part us and our tents, us and our altars, but not us and our God. (ENOT)

An alliance of kings attacked and sacked Sodom and Gomorrah. They carried off Lot and his family, as well as all his possessions.

News of this reached Abram and he launched a rescue mission. Abram's team routed the alliance's army and liberated all the people of Sodom and Gomorrah, including Lot.

On the way home, Abram met Melchizedek, the king of Salem and priest to God Most High. Melchizedek blessed Abram in the name of the Creator. Abram responded by giving the king-priest a tenth of everything. This encounter indicates that God revealed himself to people outside of Abram's family. However, the Lord set the Jews apart to be the Messiah's ethnic group.

Faith Produces Righteousness (Gen. 15:1–6)

After this, the word of the LORD came to Abram in a vision (v. 1). This time we know how God communicated with Abram. God came with words of promise and assurance based on who He is: **"I am your shield, your very great reward"** (v. 1). God was Abram's protector and rewarder. These words initiated a conversation between God and Abram.

WORDS FROM WESLEY

Genesis 15:1

After these things—(1) After that act of generous charity which Abram had done, in rescuing his neighbours, God made him this gracious visit. (2) After that victory which he had obtained over four kings; lest Abram should be too much elevated with that, God comes to tell him He had better things in store for him. . . . *Fear not Abram*—Abram might fear lest the four kings he had routed, should rally and fall upon him. No, saith God, fear not: fear not their revenge, nor thy neighbour's envy; I will take care of thee. *I am thy shield*—Or, emphatically, *I am a shield to thee*, present with thee, actually defending thee. The consideration of this, that God himself is, a shield to His people, to secure them from all destructive evils, a shield ready to them, and a shield round about them, should silence all perplexing fears. And thy exceeding great reward—Not only thy rewarder, but thy reward. God himself is the felicity of holy souls; He is the portion of their inheritance, and their cup. (ENOT)

Abram responded with a question: **"O Sovereign Lord, what can you give me since I remain childless and the one who will inherit my estate is Eliezer of Damascus?"** (v. 2). In that culture, a man with no children would give his possessions to his most faithful servant. Eliezer of Damascus was **a servant in** Abram's **household** (v. 3) who stood in line to receive the family inheritance. Sarai had always been childless (11:30), and her age (perhaps seventy-five to eighty years old) made the birth of a son seem very unlikely.

The Lord answered Abram's question with a bold statement and promise: **"This man will not be your heir, but a son coming from your own body will be your heir.... Look up at the heavens and count the stars—if indeed you can count them.... So shall your offspring be"** (15:4–5). What would Abram do in response to such a promise?

Abram believed the Lord (v. 6). Again, his faith had three sides. First, Abram believed in God's existence and the truth of His statements about himself. Second, he trusted in God's holiness and love, expecting the Lord to fulfill His promises. Third, Abram was loyal to God and obeyed Him. He did not set up a will giving everything to Eliezer. Moreover, Abram and Sarai continued trying to conceive a child.

WORDS FROM WESLEY

Genesis 15:6

Indeed, strictly speaking, the covenant of grace doth not require us to do anything at all, as absolutely and indispensably necessary in order to our justification; but only, to believe in Him who, for the sake of His Son, and the propitiation which He hath made, "justifieth the ungodly that worketh not," and imputes his faith to Him for righteousness. Even so Abraham "believed in the Lord, and he counted it to him for righteousness" (Gen. 15:6). (WJW, vol. 5, 69)

The Lord responded to Abram's faith in the same way He always responds to faith. **He credited it to** Abram **as righteousness** (v. 6). John Wesley wrote, "That is, upon the score of this he was accepted of God, and, by faith he obtained witness that he was righteous." This is God's solution to our sin problem. When we have faith, trust, believe in, and are loyal to Him, He considers us righteous.

After justifying him, the Lord reminded Abram of who He is and why He had brought Abram to this place: "I am the Lord, who brought you out of Ur of the Chaldeans to give you this land to take possession of it" (v. 7). Abram asked for assurance of God's purpose, and the Lord gave him instructions for a divided sacrifice. Abram recognized this ceremony well. The divided animals were an object lesson for the covenant. They indicated that the two parties would be cut into pieces if they failed to keep their promises.

Abram obeyed the Lord's instructions and prepared the animals. Then God did something unique. He caused Abram to fall into a deep sleep. He repeated the promises about giving Abram many descendants. The Lord added promises to Abram regarding a long life and a peaceful death. Then, God and God alone, passed between the pieces of the divided animals. The Lord independently, freely, and graciously bound himself to His covenant promise. Abram was not bound by this covenant. All he had to do was trust God to give the Promised Land to his descendants.

DISCUSSION

Discuss how God called Abram to leave home without knowing his destination. Discuss what action Abram took and what was ahead of him.

1. How do you know when the Lord is calling you to a new location or a new ministry?

2. According to Genesis 12:13, God promised to make Abram a source of blessing to "all peoples on earth." How would this blessing come to pass?

3. Read Genesis 12:4. How did Abram demonstrate his faith?

4. Suggest one way you will demonstrate your faith today.

5. Compare Genesis 12:1 and 5. Why do you agree or disagree that Abram's obedience to the Lord was incomplete?

6. According to Genesis 12:6 and 8, Abram built altars to the Lord. What does the altar represent? How can you show devotion and grateful worship to the Lord?

7. God promised Abram an heir. What circumstances might have caused Abram to doubt the fulfillment of that promise?

8. What circumstances challenge your faith today?

9. Why do you agree or disagree that the Promised Land rightfully belongs to Abram's descendants?

PRAYER

Lord, thank You for keeping Your promise to Abraham, which, from a human perspective, seemed impossible to accomplish. Let us never take our eyes off You when we are facing challenges that seem impossible to overcome.

5

GOD SEES ME

Genesis 16:1–15

God never fails to see our circumstances
and care about our well-being.

The governor of a large state cheated on his wife and fathered a child by his household maid. The affair was scandalous, of course, and the governor apologized, but the shocking event will surely continue to have negative ramifications for his family members. Of course the affair would have been even more shocking if the governor's wife had *urged* him to have a child by the maid.

This study reveals what happened when Sarai persuaded her husband Abram to father a child by her maidservant Hagar. The world is still reeling from the ensuing history of this Middle-Eastern story.

COMMENTARY

Within God's promises to make Abram into a great nation and to "bless those who bless you" and curse "whoever curses you" (Gen. 12:3) lay the hope of the ages: God called out a people through whom He would one day send a Redeemer, someone to free them from the bondage of sin.

Abram was seventy-five years old when he set out from Haran at the command of the Lord (12:4). Arriving at Shechem, he received God's promise to give the land of Canaan to him and his descendents. Sometime later God established a covenant with Abram and promised that his offspring would be as numerous as the stars in the heavens (15:5). But ten years passed, and Abram still had no children. He believed God would keep His promises, but when? How?

Here we find a dilemma that confronts many Christians. We don't understand the when and the how. And so we do whatever we can to force God's will to come to fruition. We try to do God's will our way. And it never works out quite the way we planned.

Later in its history, Israel would come to the mistaken conclusion that God cared only for His covenant people (for example, Jonah's attitude toward the Ninevites). And yet in Genesis 16 we see God's tender care and blessing on an Egyptian slave woman. She didn't have the right ancestry; she wasn't the right gender or of the right social status. But because of her relationship with Abram and his God, she was cared for and blessed by the Lord God himself.

A Misguided Wife Attempts to Fulfill God's Promise (Gen. 16:1–6)

Now Sarai, Abram's wife, had borne him no children (v. 1). Sarai (renamed Sarah in 17:15) was barren. In ancient days, the inability to have children was a disgrace; it was a sign of God's displeasure, hence Sarai's statement: **"The Lord has kept me from having children"** in 16:2. Not realizing that God's timing was meant to invoke faith, Sarai set out to rectify the problem. Her solution was a logical one: Since she could not have children herself, she would give her **maidservant** to her husband as a concubine. Because Hagar was Sarai's slave (her property), Hagar's children would also become Sarai's. This was a common custom in ancient times. It was legal, and most people would not have seen it as immoral.

Most commentators and writers focus on Sarai's sin in circumventing God's plan by offering Hagar to Abram. But that's not necessarily the case here. In 15:4, God had told Abram that "a son coming from your own body will be your heir," but no mention was made of Sarai's role. It is entirely possible that she believed God would provide a child for them, but that *she* wouldn't be part of the process. It speaks volumes for Sarai that she was willing for the promise to be fulfilled without her being part of the blessing. It could be viewed as an act of humility on her part. She wanted God's will to be done more than she wanted the privilege of carrying the child herself.

WORDS FROM WESLEY

Genesis 16:1

We have here the marriage of Abram to Hagar, who was his secondary wife. Herein, though he may be excused, he cannot be justified; for from the beginning it was not so: and when it was so, it seems to have proceeded from an irregular desire to build up their families, for the speedier peopling of the world. But now we must not do so? Christ has reduced this matter to the first institution, and makes the marriage union to be between one man and one woman only. (ENOT)

And let's not forget that she and her husband had already **been living in Canaan ten years** (16:3). She and Abram were well advanced in years already. Maybe, after years of patient waiting, she came to the realization that perhaps God wanted her to *do* something. We fall into this trap all the time. "God helps those who help themselves," we rationalize. And so we think we have to *do* something in order to make God's promises come true. We can hardly blame Sarai for being logical at this point!

But let's not forget Abram's role here. Sarai said, **"Go, sleep with my maidservant; perhaps I can build a family through her"** (v. 2). Did you notice Abram's response? Moses simply recorded for us that **Abram agreed to what Sarai said** (v. 2). If his wife was wavering in her faith, this is where Abram could have encouraged her. He should have affirmed his devotion to her and refused. Maybe that's what Sarai was hoping for. Instead, he agreed to her proposal.

It is hard to miss the similarities between this story and the story of Adam and Eve in Genesis 3. Eve saw the fruit and reasoned that it was harmless. She wanted something for herself that God had not yet given, and she found a shortcut to get what she wanted now. Once she ate, she gave it to her husband (who could have stopped her from eating the fruit in the first place), and he ate. Abram agreed. Satan's strategy for circumventing God's plans had not changed. And God's people were ensnared again.

Abram **slept with Hagar, and she conceived** (16:4). The plan worked, but everything did not work out as Sarai had expected. **When** Hagar **knew she was pregnant, she began to despise her mistress** (v. 4). Perhaps Hagar made comments to remind Sarai of her barrenness or insinuated that she was dearer to Abram than Sarai was because she was carrying his child. Whatever the exchange, Sarai went to her husband with the problem. She put the blame squarely on him: **"You are responsible for the wrong I am suffering. . . . May the LORD judge between you and me"** (v. 5).

WORDS FROM WESLEY

Genesis 16:4

We have here the ill consequences of Abram's marriage to Hagar: a deal of mischief it made presently. Hagar no sooner perceives herself with child, but she looks scornfully upon her mistress; upbraids her perhaps with her barrenness, and insults over her. Sarai falls upon Abram, and very unjustly charges him with the injury, suspecting that he countenanced Hagar's insolence: and as one not willing to hear what Abram had to say she rashly appeals to God. *The Lord judge between me and thee*, as if Abram had refused to right her. When passion is upon the throne, reason is out of doors, and is neither heard nor spoken. Those are not always in the right that are most forward in appealing to God. Rash and bold imprecations are commonly evidences of guilt and a bad cause. (ENOT)

Reading the story, most of us would think, "*She* is responsible for the wrong she's suffering; it was *her* idea." But it is human nature to try to blame someone else for our own poor decisions and choices. After all, Abram was partly to blame for agreeing to the scheme in the first place. And, seeing the situation, he apparently had made no effort to try to correct the growing rift between Sarai and Hagar. Abram couldn't claim it wasn't his problem. If it was happening in his household, he was responsible.

Abram's response was unfortunate. Instead of taking control of the situation, he left it for Sarai to handle: **Do with her whatever you think best** (v. 6). In his defense, he may have felt he had no choice. Having taken Hagar as his wife (v. 3, which would be better translated as "concubine"), he had divided loyalties and didn't know how to satisfy both women. But his decision had disastrous consequences: **Then Sarai mistreated Hagar; so she fled from her** (v. 6).

A Mistreated Servant Attests to God's Faithfulness (Gen. 16:7–15)

Hagar is the most sympathetic character in this story, but perhaps also the most culpable. She was a slave, little more than a piece of property, probably given to Sarai by Pharaoh when she was taken into his palace to be his wife (12:10–20, another instance when Abram showed an incredible lack of wisdom). Hagar had no choice in this scenario. She became pregnant, knowing the baby would not even be considered her own. It must have been a bitter experience indeed!

But life is full of its bitter experiences, full of circumstances beyond our control. Our response in the midst of them is what is supremely important. In the New Testament, Paul told those who found themselves serving as slaves to be the best slaves they could be (see Eph. 6:5–6; Col. 3:22–24). He certainly didn't condone the social institution of slavery, but he gave guidelines for righteous behavior for those who find themselves on the "wrong" end of the social order.

Hagar didn't respond the way she should have. She despised (or cursed) her mistress. When she was treated harshly, she ran away, leaving Abram's family and Abram's God. She could have made the situation better, but she chose to make it worse. But thankfully, there is a God who specializes in cleaning up the messes we sometimes make, a God who cares enough to help us put the pieces back together.

In Genesis 16:7, we see the first instance of an angelic appearance in the Bible: **The angel of the LORD found Hagar near a spring in the desert**. God, in His grace, sought out Hagar. She was on a dangerous trip back to Egypt (**beside the road to Shur**, which was near the border of Egypt; see 25:18). In her condition, she probably would not have survived the trip through the desert. Her situation was desperate.

WORDS FROM WESLEY

Genesis 16:7

Here is the first mention we have in Scripture of an angel's appearance, who arrested her in her flight. It should seem she was making towards her own country, for she was in the way to Shur, which lay towards Egypt. 'Twere well if our afflictions would make us think of our home, the better county. But Hagar was now out of the way of her duty, and going farther astray, when the angel found her. It is a great mercy to be stopt in a sinful way, either by conscience or providence. (ENOT)

The angel (literally "messenger") addressed her as **"Hagar, servant of Sarai"** (16:8), reminding her of her position and obligation to her mistress, but also assuring her that God knew her name and situation (see John 10:3). The angel asked simply, **"Where have you come from, and where are you going?"** (Gen.

16:8). Again, notice the similarity to the Adam and Eve story in Genesis 3. After they sinned, God sought them out in the garden and asked, "Where are you?" and "Who told you . . . ?" However, unlike Adam, who hid, Hagar was completely transparent with her answer: **"I'm running away from my mistress Sarai"** (16:8).

The blessing given by the angel to Hagar in verse 10 was contingent on her obedience to his command in verse 9: **"Go back to your mistress and submit to her."** In 12:3, God had promised that those who blessed Abram's family would be blessed, and those who cursed it would be cursed. Interestingly, the Hebrew word used for "despise" (*qalal*) in verses 4–5 is the same word translated "curse" in 12:3 and also in Deuteronomy 23:5. Even though Hagar was an Egyptian (a fact mentioned twice for emphasis in Gen. 16:1 and 3), she would still be blessed if she submitted to God's covenant people, even as she was currently paying the consequences for having cursed them.

WORDS FROM WESLEY
Genesis 16:11

Ishmael, that is, God will hear; and the reason is, because the Lord hath heard: He hath, and therefore He will. The experience we have had of God's seasonable kindness in distress should encourage us to hope for the like help in the like exigencies. Even there, where there is little cry of devotion, the God of pity hears the cry of affliction: tears speak as well as prayers. (ENOT)

The angel foretold the birth of her son, whom she was to name **Ishmael** (v. 11), meaning "God hears." He would become a great nation (16:10; see also 17:20), but he would be **a wild donkey of a man; his hand will be against everyone . . . and he will live in hostility toward all his brothers** (16:12). Ishmael and his descendents would roam the desert as Bedouins, untamable and hostile. It was the Ishmaelites who purchased Joseph as a slave and took him to Egypt (Gen. 37:27). To this day their descendents, Arabs, continue to live in hostility toward the people of Israel.

Hagar's response to this revelation was to name the well beside which she sat in honor of God. **She gave this name to the LORD who spoke to her: "You are the God who sees me"** (16:13). Moses told us it was **the LORD** (YHWH) who spoke to her. God himself was the One who saw her in her affliction and came to her aid. The well and the son in her womb would be a testimony that the Lord sees and hears.

If God could hear and see the affliction (see v. 11, also Ex. 2:24; 3:16) of an Egyptian slave, how much more would He hear and see the affliction of His covenant people? This must have been a startling lesson for Abram and Sarai when Hagar returned with this story of God's mercy and care. **So Hagar bore Abram a son, and Abram gave the name Ishmael to the son she had borne** (Gen. 16:15).

WORDS FROM WESLEY

Genesis 16:14

The well was called Beer-lahai-roi—The well of him that lives and sees me. 'Tis likely Hagar put this name upon it, and it was retained long after. This was the place where the God of glory manifested the special care He took of a poor woman in distress. Those that are graciously admitted into communion with God, and receive seasonable comforts from Him, should tell others what He has done for their souls, that they also may be encouraged to seek Him and trust in Him. (ENOT)

God was aware of Abram and Sarai's situation. He heard the cries of their hearts. He saw their pain. And He would answer . . . in another thirteen years. No doubt Hagar's testimony of God's faithfulness was an encouragement to them as they waited patiently for the fulfillment of God's promise.

DISCUSSION

If satellites view Earth in clear detail, we shouldn't question the fact that God sees us clearly. But do we grasp the fact that He sees our individual situation and personal needs clearly? This study focuses on God's personal interest in His children.

1. Is anyone beyond God's love and care because of his or her status in life? Why or why not?

2. Sarai said, "The Lord has kept me from having children" (Gen. 16:2). Do you think she was resentful that she was childless? Why or why not?

3. Read Genesis 16:3. What is your opinion of the plan Sarai suggested to Abram?

4. Have you ever grown tired of waiting for the Lord to keep a promise? Describe the situation.

5. What characteristic do you think Abram displayed when he consented to Sarai's plan? If you think he acted wrongly, what action do you think he should have taken?

6. What characteristics would you ascribe to an ideal spouse?

7. Read Genesis 16:6. What flaws, if any, do you see in Abram's character? In Sarai's character?

8. Why do you agree or disagree that marriage should be monogamous?

9. How does God's treatment of runaway Hagar encourage you?

PRAYER

Lord, give us patience as we wait for the fulfillment of Your promises in our lives. Give us the courage and fortitude to wait for Your perfect timing.

6

GOD'S PROTECTION IS STILL AVAILABLE

Genesis 13:8–13; 18:20–25; 19:15–17, 29

God protects His own.

The cartoon strip *Pickles* showed Earl refusing to lend his good rake to a neighbor. Instead, he offered the neighbor a toothless old rake, explaining that people forget to return what they borrow. Later, Earl's wife reprimanded him and asked where he had acquired such a useless old rake. After thinking awhile, Earl remembered he had borrowed it from his neighbor when it was new. He had forgotten to return it and had worn it out.

Unlike Earl, Abraham was willing to give the best pasture to Lot rather than create hard feelings between the two. This study focuses on Abraham's unselfishness and subsequent events.

COMMENTARY

The context of these passages is relationships in the midst of uncertainty. Genesis 12 begins with the Lord saying to Abram, "Leave your country, your people and your father's household and go to the land I will show you" (12:1). Abram was removed from everything and everyone he knew. He became the minority in his culture, his language, and his worldview. Since these are our primary tools in making decisions, from a human perspective, Abram was at a disadvantage wherever he went.

Abram's advantage, which he had to learn to understand and use, was God's promise. In 12:2–3, God said to Abram, "I will make you into a great nation and I will bless you; I will make your name great, and you will be a blessing. I will bless those who bless you, and whoever curses you I will curse; and all peoples on earth will be blessed through you."

Like many of us, Abram did not understand the full implications of God's promise. He continued to make decisions based on human terms. However, as the story of Abram progresses, we see Abram making better and more mature decisions. Unfortunately, the narrative does not reveal how much the promise of God factored into those decisions.

This study's focus is "God protects His own." That is a relational statement designed to instill in us the confidence that God is on our side. Paul put it this way: "Those he [God] predestined, he also called; those he called, he also justified; those he justified, he also glorified. What, then, shall we say in response to this? If God is for us, who can be against us?" (Rom. 8:30–31).

Therefore, we must not only see these verses in the context of Abram's life, but also in the context of our own lives. The story of Abram is given to us so that we might see ourselves in him and see the God who made promises and acted on behalf of Abram as the same God who makes promises to us and acts on our behalf. As Christians, we too have been called to leave the world and its pattern of making decisions. Like Abram we have been given a divine promise—God's salvation. Like Abram, we must learn to make decisions in the uncertainty of our lives in relationship to God and His promise.

Generosity, Selflessness, Temptation, and Sin (Gen. 13:8–13)

In this part of the story, Abram was certain of his relationship to Lot, **"For we are brothers"** (v. 8), Abram said. He was uncertain of the future, but he was certain that the present circumstance was threatening a relationship he held dear. Besides Sarai, Lot was the only relative who left Ur with Abram. Lot meant more to Abram than his future or his fortune. Abram made this point when he asked Lot, **"Is not the whole land before *you*?"**

(v. 9, emphasis added). Abram gave Lot the full choice of where to move his family and his herd. **"If you go to the left,"** Abram told Lot, **"I'll go to the right; if you go to the right, I'll go to the left."** Abram's concern was that there would be no quarreling between them. It did not matter to Abram if that goal cost him everything he had.

Here is a place where we would like to know how much Abram's faith in God's provision for his future affected his attitude toward Lot. Maybe it is better that we do not know. It may be that we can use the promise of God for selfish reasons if we are not careful. Abram is presented here as one with a pure motive. Not even the promise of God's blessing was in his mind. His sole concern was his relationship with Lot. The high value Abram placed on another person is the same value we should place on one another. Again, Paul wrote, "Nobody should seek his own good, but the good of others" (1 Cor. 10:24), and "Do nothing out of selfish ambition or vain conceit, but in humility consider others better than yourselves. Each of you should look not only to your own interests, but also to the interests of others" (Phil. 2:3–4).

Lot is presented in opposition to these principles. Lot's only concern was his future and his fortune. The phrase "whole plain" is used to emphasize this in Genesis 13:10–11. Lot saw the whole plain of the Jordan and became greedy. While it is true that Abram and Lot were too close together for the size of their flocks and herds, the passage seems to suggest that "the whole plain of the Jordan" may have had enough room to share. Or, at the very least, Lot did not need the whole plain for himself. He could have left some of it for Abram, and he would still have had plenty of room.

The result was that **Abram lived in the land of Canaan, while Lot lived among the cities of the plain and pitched his tents near Sodom** (v. 12). Lot's greed and selfishness led him into the lion's den of temptation, while Abram's generosity and selflessness led him away to safety. Ultimately, this is an early example of Jesus' teaching: "Whoever tries to keep his life will lose it, and whoever loses his life will preserve it" (Luke 17:33).

WORDS FROM WESLEY

Genesis 13:11–13

We have no account of their [the people of Noah's day] reforming their ways, of any universal or general repentance, before God separated Abraham to himself, to be the father of His chosen people (Gen. 12:1, 2). Nor is there any reason to believe, that the rest of mankind were improved either in wisdom or virtue, when "Lot and Abraham separated themselves, and Lot pitched his tent toward Sodom" (Gen. 13:11, 12). Of those among whom he dwelt it is particularly remarked, "The men of Sodom" (and of all "the cities of the plain") "were wicked and sinners before the Lord exceedingly" (Gen. 13:13); so that not even "ten righteous persons" could be found among them: The consequence of which was, that "the Lord rained upon them brimstone and fire from the Lord out of heaven" (Gen. 19:24). (WJW, vol. 9, 198)

Connecting the Fairness of God to the Presence of God (Gen. 18:20–25)

This part of the story begins with an interesting twist. **Then the LORD said, "The outcry against Sodom and Gomorrah is so great and their sin so grievous that I will go down and see if what they have done is as bad as the outcry that has reached me. If not, I will know"** (vv. 20–21). It is important here to see the God of Abraham as a personal God, one who is personally involved in judging the sins of humanity. This differs from other religions of the day that viewed God as an unconcerned deity who was removed from the daily lives of people.

In the text, verse 22 reads, **The men turned away and went toward Sodom, but Abraham remained standing before the**

LORD. However, there are other ancient Hebrew documents of Genesis that read "but the Lord remained standing before Abraham." This reading seems to fit better since the other men (angels) went to Sodom. So the Lord delayed His personal visit to Sodom in order to engage Abraham in this conversation.

WORDS FROM WESLEY

Genesis 18:19

*I know Abraham that he will command his children, and his household after him—*This is a bright part of Abraham's character. He not only prayed with his family, but he taught them, as a man of knowledge; nay, he commanded them as a man in authority, and was prophet and king, as well as priest, in his own house. And he not only took care of his children, but of his household: his servants were catechized servants. Masters of families should instruct, and inspect the manners of all under their roof. And this is given as the reason why God would make known to him His purpose concerning Sodom; because He was communicative of His knowledge, and improved it for the benefit of those that were under His charge. (ENOT)

Since the Lord stayed and Abraham knew that Lot was in Sodom, he approached the Lord and said, **"Will you sweep away the righteous with the wicked?"** (v. 23). We are not to assume that Abraham considered Lot righteous. Nor are we to assume that Abraham knew there were righteous people in Sodom. This conversation is an example of the ancient interest in philosophical dialogue that addressed real-life questions. The ancient peoples did not make the same distinction between theory and practice that we do today. They understood almost all actions to be based upon some philosophy of life.

Abraham's entire conversation with the Lord, which extends through verse 33, is based upon his philosophy—or more correctly, his theology—that **the Judge of all the earth** will **do right** (v. 25). Abraham's conviction on this point may have stemmed from God's presence in his life. Abraham had witnessed firsthand the goodness of God. God continued to bless Abraham even when he strayed from the will of God. Figuratively, Abraham had been the righteous one in the midst of Sodom. In other words, Abraham had received God's grace and now was pleading for the same grace to be bestowed upon others.

The principle behind Abraham's opinion of God is that God values the relationship He has with the righteous over the punishment deserved by the wicked. Thus, a verse such as "He causes his sun to rise on the evil and the good, and sends rain on the righteous and the unrighteous" (Matt. 5:45) should not be viewed as a lack of justice, but as evidence of God's grace available to us all. God judges fairly, not simply because He is God, but because He is present and views the unrighteousness for himself. Even then, if God desires it, grace may abound. For that we must praise His name!

Our Action in the Midst of God's Salvation and Punishment (Gen. 19:15–17, 29)

The phrase **with the coming of dawn** (v. 15) does more than set the time for this story. In the Bible, light symbolizes the time for action. Jesus said, "A man who walks by day will not stumble, for he sees by this world's light. It is when he walks by night that he stumbles, for he has no light" (John 11:9–10). And again, "I have come into the world as a light, so that no one who believes in me should stay in darkness" (12:46). The coming of dawn symbolizes the coming of the revelation that God was about to bring judgment and the coming of God's grace as safety for those who would heed the warning.

When God's will is revealed, action is necessary. Lot was instructed to take his wife and two daughters **who are here** (Gen. 19:15). Lot's sons-in-law had been given the opportunity to go as well, but they laughed at Lot. Their fate reminds us of the lament Jesus gave over Jerusalem as He entered the city for the last time on a donkey: "They will not leave one stone on another, because you did not recognize the time of God's coming to you" (Luke 19:44). While God's punishment and destruction of sin is inevitable, anyone who hears God's warning and acts on it will be saved. If you do not move, you will be swept away.

WORDS FROM WESLEY

Genesis 19:17

Look not behind thee—He must not loiter by the way; *stay not in all the plain*—For it would all be made one dead sea: he must not take up short of the place of refuge appointed him; *escape to the mountain*—Such as these are the commands given to those who through grace are delivered out of a sinful state. 1. Return not to sin and Satan, for that's looking back to Sodom. 2. Rest not in the world, for that's staying in the plain. And, 3. Reach toward Christ and heaven, for that is escaping to the mountain, short of which we must not take up. (ENOT)

When Lot hesitated, the angels of the Lord took the four people by the hands and **led them safely out of the city, for the LORD was merciful to them** (Gen. 19:16). Lot and his family felt the same twinge of doubt we experience when God calls us to leave the security of what we know for the uncertainty of a holy life we do not know. Can it really be so bad? Would God really punish you for staying? Notice that while the angels led them safely out of the city, Lot and his family still had choices to make. They still had to run away from the city, and they could not look back or stop. Their first instructions were to flee to the mountains, but they were afraid because all they knew was city life. So, again, God had mercy on them and allowed them to go to a small town. Thus, the picture we get of God's mercy is that any action on our part toward God will be repaid by an abundance of untiring mercy. Our responsibility is so small compared to God's that it seems insignificant. This is the deception. Though we are small and have little power, God has placed eternal significance on anything we can do, hence the parable of the mustard seed (see Luke 13:19; 17:6).

Genesis 19:29 brings to light another action that we can accomplish in the midst of God's salvation and punishment. We can pray for the salvation of others. Lot never seemed to be righteous. God did not spare the cities, so evidently He did not find any righteousness. He brought Lot out, not because of his righteousness, but because of the faithfulness of Abraham toward Lot. Paul wrote an interesting concept to the Corinthians: "For the unbelieving husband has been sanctified through his wife, and the unbelieving wife has been sanctified through her believing husband. Otherwise your children would be unclean, but as it is, they are holy" (1 Cor. 7:13–14). We must understand salvation and holiness in terms of our relationships to others as well as in terms of our relationship to God. Abraham's relationship to God saved Lot and his family from destruction. "The prayer of a righteous man is powerful and effective" (James 5:16). Again, life is uncertain, so we must learn to trust in the Lord with all our heart and lean not on our own understanding (see Prov. 3:5).

WORDS FROM WESLEY

Genesis 19:29

God remembered Abraham, and for his sake *sent Lot out of the overthrow*—God will certainly give an answer of peace to the prayer of faith in His own way and time. (ENOT)

DISCUSSION

Discuss how we can trust God to protect us even when we risk financial loss by placing a higher value on relationships than possessions. This study shows what happened when Abram chose to honor a relationship that involved material loss.

1. Read Genesis 13:1–4. How do you know Abram's prosperity did not weaken his devotion to the Lord?

2. What warning about riches do you find in 1 Timothy 6:17?

3. Do you think it is harder for a rich person or a poor person to trust in the Lord? Defend your answer.

4. What kinds of issues might divide members of God's family? Why is it necessary to "make every effort to keep the unity of the Spirit" (see Eph. 4:3)?

5. Read Genesis 13:10–12. What bad choices did Lot make?

6. Is it easier to maintain a righteous life: (A) in a rural area rather than in an urban area, (B) in a city rather than in a village, or (C) neither since a righteous life is not affected by where a person lives? Explain your answer.

7. How does Abraham's intercession for Sodom encourage you to pray?

8. How does what eventually happened to Lot motivate you to make wise choices?

PRAYER

Lord, give us the ability to be a peace with all people, at least as far as it depends on us. Give us the humility to pursue reconciliation in the presence of conflict.

GOD PROVIDES OUR FUTURE

Genesis 22:1–18

God will provide when we are fully and
totally surrendered to His will.

Reportedly, when the offering plate was passed to a tightfisted church member, he would drop fifty cents into the plate and sing under his breath, "When we asunder part, it gives me inward pain." We can only wonder what he might sing under his breath if he thought a voice from heaven summoned him to drop one hundred dollars into the plate. Would he sing, "Rescue the perishing"?

One hundred dollars is simply a drop in the bucket compared to what God told Abraham to present as an offering to Him. He commanded Abraham to sacrifice Isaac, his only son, as an offering. This study discloses Abraham's response and what followed his response.

COMMENTARY

In Genesis 15:4–6, God promised Abraham that He would give him a son whose descendants would be as numerous as the stars. At that time, Abraham was ninety years of age, and his wife, Sarah, had been unable to bear children.

After time passed, recorded in chapter 16, Sarah assumed she could never bear children at her advanced age. She gave her Egyptian maidservant named Hagar to Abraham to bear children for her as was the custom in that time. In due course, Ishmael was born, the father of today's Arab nations.

Chapter 18 records the coming of three visitors to see Abraham. "Then the LORD said, 'I will surely return to you about this time next year, and Sarah your wife will have a son'" (v. 10). Sarah heard those words and "laughed to herself" (v. 12). But Abraham believed after the Lord said, "Is anything too hard for the LORD?" (v. 14).

In chapter 21, Isaac was born. "Abraham was a hundred years old when his son Isaac was born to him" (v. 5). Sarah exulted, "God has brought me laughter, and everyone who hears about this will laugh with me. . . . Who would have said to Abraham that Sarah would nurse children? Yet I have borne him a son in his old age" (vv. 6–7).

The words "some time later" suggest that possibly several years had passed since Isaac was born. We cannot be certain how old Isaac was, but he was old enough to carry a heavy load of wood for the burnt offering. Possibly he was a strong, young teenage boy, able to assist his father in this way.

Terrifying Test (Gen. 22:1–2)

God told Abraham, **"Take your son, your only son, Isaac, whom you love. . . . Sacrifice him there as a burnt offering"** (22:2). Those words, **your son . . . only son . . . whom you love** are poignant words for a man who waited ten years for Isaac to be born following God's promise when he was ninety years old. Given all the things God had promised Abraham about future generations that were to come through his son, the instruction to offer him up as a burnt offering doesn't seem on the surface to be realistic.

Perhaps you have had an impression through the Holy Spirit to do something that didn't make sense to you. Possibly you began to question whether, after all, it was God speaking. What God said through the prophet Isaiah may help us: "As the heavens are higher than the earth, so are my ways higher than your ways, and my thoughts [higher] than your thoughts" (Isa. 55:9). According to these words, we should not expect to always understand the concept and outcomes when God prompts us to do something that seems unlikely for us to accomplish.

The principle we learn from this passage is that God doesn't make mistakes. He may surprise us, even shock us, with what He asks us to do. But He's always right. It always works out for our best and for His glory.

WORDS FROM WESLEY
Genesis 22:1

Here is the trial of Abraham's faith, whether it continued so strong, so vigorous, so victorious, after a long settlement in communion with God, as it was at first, when by it he left his country: then it appeared that he loved God better than his father; now, that he loved Him better than his son. *After these things* — After all the other exercises he had had, all the difficulties he had gone through: now perhaps he was beginning to think the storms were blown over; but after all, this encounter comes, which is sharper than any yet. *God did tempt Abraham* — Not to draw him to sin, so Satan tempts; but to discover his graces, how strong they were, that they might be found to praise and honour and glory. (ENOT)

We need to deal with a seeming contradiction in these verses. In speaking to Abraham, God referred to Isaac as **your only son** (Gen. 22:2). But what about Ishmael? Was he not also a son of Abraham? Although Ishmael was indeed also a son of Abraham, he was not the son of promise. Likely this was the context of God's words to Abraham. However, God did not ignore Ishmael. He spoke to his mother, Hagar, these words of promise: "I will make him into a great nation" (Gen. 21:18).

Instant Obedience (Gen. 22:3–5)

Abraham was a man of faith. Human as he was, he believed in God and left the outcome in his hands. Eager to obey God, **early the next morning Abraham got up and saddled his donkey** (v. 3). He set off on a three-day journey with Isaac and two of his servants, but not before careful preparation of cutting wood for the burnt offering.

Three days into the journey, Abraham **saw the place in the distance** (v. 4). The rugged trip wasn't over, but it was time to leave the two young men behind to care for the donkey. He and Isaac went on.

The words **"I and the boy"** apply to the following subject and verbs: **"We will worship and then we *will come back to you*"** (v. 5, emphasis added). But what about God's command to offer Isaac as a burnt offering? Abraham, noted for his faith, believed God would follow through on His promise that through Isaac many descendants would come. Just how that would happen Abraham left in the hands of God.

The writer of Hebrews spelled it out: "Abraham reasoned that God could raise the dead, and figuratively speaking he did receive Isaac back from death" (Heb. 11:19). This, written under inspiration of the Holy Spirit, helps explain what was going through Abraham's mind as he and Isaac set out for that distant place of sacrifice.

The calm deliberation with which Abraham went about obeying God is startling. We can learn a great deal from Abraham's actions. Instant obedience is a sure way to fulfill God's will in our lives. Delayed obedience sometimes results in missing the opportunity God wanted us to respond to. Delayed obedience may become disobedience and defeat God's purposes. Instant obedience honors God and fulfills His purposes.

Burden Bearer (Gen. 22:6)

Abraham took the wood for the burnt offering and placed it on his son Isaac (v. 6). As we move through this chapter, we realize that Isaac, who was announced to become a burnt offering upon an altar, represented Christ, the Lamb of God, who died for our sins upon the cross. The parallel here is striking.

Following His brutal beatings at the hands of Roman soldiers, Jesus lost a great deal of blood. Yet, He was forced to carry a heavy wooden cross toward the site of His sacrificial death.

No doubt, the amount of wood Isaac carried on his back as he headed with his father to the place of his impending sacrificial death was also a heavy load. The amount of wood needed for such a sacrifice was significant. Yet Isaac carried it without complaint. He complied with the instructions of his father.

Natural Question; Supernatural Answer (Gen. 22:7–8)

As Abraham and Isaac continued their trek through rugged terrain, Isaac was thinking. Everything didn't add up. Always before, when a sacrifice was to be made, his father carefully examined many animals to find a perfect one. What about that missing ingredient?

Isaac asked his father, **"The fire and wood are here . . . but where is the lamb?"** (v. 7). The situation didn't make sense. Isaac was confused. His father had not told him what God had asked him to do. How could they sacrifice without an animal?

WORDS FROM WESLEY

Genesis 22:8

My son, God will provide himself a lamb—This was the language either, 1. Of his obedience; we must offer the lamb which God has appointed now to be offered; thus giving Him this general rule of submission to the divine will to prepare Him for the application of it to himself. Or, 2. Of his faith; whether he meant it so or no, this proved to be the meaning of it; a sacrifice was provided instead of Isaac. Thus 1. Christ the great sacrifice of atonement was of God's providing: when none in heaven or earth could have found a lamb for that burnt-offering, God himself found the ransom. 2. All our sacrifices of acknowledgement are of God's providing too; 'tis He that prepares the heart. The broken and contrite spirit is a sacrifice of God, of His providing. (ENOT)

Abraham's answer was profound: **"God himself will provide the lamb"** (v. 8). Notice that Abraham did not say God would supply *a* lamb. He used the definite article; God would supply *the* lamb. That seemed to satisfy Isaac, for the verse continues by saying that **the two of them went on together.**

Obviously, Abraham's faith in God had been transmitted to his son. Abraham spoke words of faith, and Isaac, too, believed.

The Deadly Deed (Gen. 22:9–10)

When father and son arrived at their destination, Abraham built an altar and arranged the wood upon it while Isaac looked on. Then, for Isaac, the unexpected happened. Abraham **bound his son Isaac and laid him on the altar, on top of the wood** (v. 9).

We are given no record of conversation between father and son. Neither is any hint given that Isaac resisted. With Abraham being one hundred years old and Isaac being a strong young man, very likely Isaac could have escaped his father's grasp and run faster than Abraham. He could have run away. Jesus could have escaped the cross, too, but He didn't. Isaac lay upon the wood on the altar as a willing sacrifice. Abraham **took the knife to slay his son** (v. 10). His intent was clear to Isaac. It was also clear to God.

Crisis Intervention (Gen. 22:11–12)

Just as Abraham was about to do the unthinkable, a voice from heaven called Abraham by name, telling him to spare his son. The voice's message was clear: **"Now I know that you fear God"** (v. 12). Because of Abraham's obedience, his faith and integrity were certain. Those words **"Now I know"** have intrigued readers of the Bible for many centuries. Didn't God know how Abraham would respond before He issued the incredible command? God said through Isaiah, "I am God, and there is none like me. I make known the end from the beginning, from ancient times, what is still to come" (Isa. 46:9–10).

Did God test Abraham for God's benefit or for Abraham's? When God said, **"Now I know"** (Gen. 22:12), was He affirming himself or Abraham? Given the words of God in Isaiah 46, one may conclude that this test was to strengthen the already considerable faith of this godly man. It shows beyond doubt that no matter what God asks us to do, obedience pays rich dividends.

WORDS FROM WESLEY

Genesis 22:8

Safely we may our Isaacs give,
And leave them on the altar laid:
If best for us that they should live,
A way for their deliverance made
Shall lift our hearts to things above,
And perfect us in heavenly love. (PW, vol. 9, 24)

Plentiful Provision (Gen. 22:13–14)

Once God halted the sacrifice of Isaac, Abraham spied a ram with its horns caught in some bushes. After unbinding Isaac and setting him free, Abraham took the ram, bound it, laid it upon the altar, and offered up to God a burnt offering.

At last, the lamb spoken of by Abraham had come. And later the Lamb of God made the ultimate sacrifice for the sins of the world.

Covenant Blessing (Gen. 22:15–18)

Notice in verses 15–16 that the writer referred to the one speaking to Abraham as **the angel of the LORD** as well as **the LORD**. Throughout the chapters of Genesis dealing with the life of Abraham, these terms are used interchangeably. The great "I AM" was there on the scene as Abraham passed the most difficult test of his life.

What did the Lord say? **"I swear by myself . . . that because you have done this . . . I will surely bless you and make your descendants as numerous as the stars . . . and as the sand on the seashore"** (vv. 16–17). Even more importantly the Lord promised, **"Through your offspring all nations on earth will be blessed, because you have obeyed me"** (v. 18). The apostle Paul made clear in Galatians 3:16 that the word *offspring*, or literally "seed," which is a singular word, referred specifically to Christ. As is often the case, the Bible interprets itself.

WORDS FROM WESLEY

Genesis 22:16

"Thy seed shall possess the gate of his enemies, because thou hast obeyed my voice." Here Abraham's obedience, that is, the result of it, is imputed to his posterity. (WJW, vol. 9, 395)

Does it pay to obey God even when the outcome seems questionable? Abraham would tell you yes. In the words of the hymn writer, "It pays to serve Jesus, it pays every day; it pays every step of the way." It pays even when that step is a step of faith.

DISCUSSION

Discuss if your love for God exceeds the love you feel for even your closest loved one. Abraham's love for God was tested when God instructed him to sacrifice his only son Isaac as a burnt offering.

1. How did you first learn that God sacrificed His Son for you?

2. Read 1 John 4:19. What prompted you to love God? What keeps that love alive and growing?

3. What impresses you most about Abraham's character?

4. What impresses you most about Isaac's character?

5. What impresses you most about God's character?

6. Read Romans 12:1–2. What is each believer called upon to sacrifice to God? Why do you agree or disagree that this should be a one-time sacrifice?

7. Why do you agree or disagree that Abraham displayed faith when he promised he and his son would return to his two servants (Gen. 22:5)?

8. Read John 15:2 and 13. How can believers best prove to unbelievers that believers truly love the Lord and one another?

PRAYER

Lord, give us the fortitude to faithfully endure any test You allow in our lives, and the wisdom to accurately interpret the results of those tests.

8

SEEK GOD'S BEST

Genesis 25:29–34; 27:6–10, 30–31, 34–35

God's blessing is of greater value than
physical and material abundance.

Siblings differ from each other, and sometimes the differences
are huge.

Fred became a burly football player. His brother Howard was
scrawny and delicate. He showed no interest in sports, but he
loved to crochet. Caley and her sister Cathy took piano lessons
for a year, but Caley splashed tears all over the keyboard when
she practiced. However, Cathy loved to practice and play the
piano. Her mother could hardly tear her away from the instrument
for dinner. Sibling differences do not have to divide a family, but
sibling rivalry can seriously damage family relationships.

This study shows how sibling rivalry divided Isaac and
Rebekah's family.

COMMENTARY

Jacob and Esau, like most of us, were products of their family
system, genetics, and environment. What separated them from
each other was the value they placed on the blessing of God.

Abraham was Jacob and Esau's grandfather. He is known as
the father of the Hebrew people. He grew up in a pagan nation,
in the midst of an idol-worshiping family. But God met with
Abraham, and he learned to walk with God. Abraham's main fear
was that all this wealth would go to someone who was not a
descendant, for he was childless (Gen. 15:2–3). But God promised
that Abraham would be the father of a great nation.

Naturally, this was impossible because Abraham and his wife Sarah were too old to have children. But God kept His word. When Abraham was one hundred and Sarah was ninety years old, they had a son. They named him Isaac (Gen. 21).

The blessing of God rested on Abraham in such a way that he was given wealth. He was given a son whom God promised to make into a great nation. He was given a promise by God that Abraham's descendants would inherit the land he lived in. He was given revelation so that he might know God. This blessing was Abraham's real wealth, and it was to be passed down the family line.

That, however, was not the only thing that was passed down. Abraham had a tendency to lie, or at least, not tell the whole truth when he was in danger (Gen. 12; 20). Abraham's wife Sarah was beautiful. She was so beautiful, in fact, that Abraham was worried the king would kill him to possess Sarah. So he told Sarah to introduce herself as Abraham's brother. This lie brought them into some difficult situations in which God intervened.

Isaac, Abraham's son, not only inherited Abraham's wealth, but he also inherited the blessing of God given to Abraham and his descendants. In fact, the blessing of God rested on Isaac in such a way that his crops and herds increased exponentially (Gen. 26:12–14). But he also inherited this ability to lie (Gen. 26). He told the exact same lie, to a different king, for the same reason.

Isaac and his wife Rebekah had twins. The older one was named Esau; the younger one, born grasping the heel of his brother, was named Jacob. Esau grew up to be a "man's man." He was a hunter, an archer, and an outdoorsman. Isaac loved his wild game and loved Esau for bringing it to him. Esau was Isaac's favorite son. Jacob was a quiet man. He stayed around the tents. He was Rebekah's favorite son (Gen. 25:28).

It was the practice of ancient Middle-Eastern culture for the oldest son to inherit a double portion of the father's estate. It would be the expectation for the oldest son to carry on the family line. In the case of Jacob and Esau, the cultural expectation would be for Esau to inherit two-thirds of his father's estate and Jacob would receive one-third of the estate. But it also seems that the blessing of God, promised to Abraham and passed to Isaac, was only going to be passed to one of these sons. Esau would be the traditional choice to inherit this blessing.

Jacob and Esau were growing up in a wealthy family. This family was blessed by God yet prone to deception. The boys were prone to competition. One boy was his mother's favorite, and the other boy was his father's favorite. There was an estate at stake as well as the blessing of God. This is where we pick up the story.

Esau Despised His Birthright (Gen. 25:29–34)

The Bible doesn't tell us how old Jacob and Esau were when this story happened. Genesis 25:27 refers to them as men. This probably means that they were at least teenagers. They were old enough for Jacob to understand the meaning of birthright and young enough for Esau to think the future was irrelevant.

WORDS FROM WESLEY

Genesis 25:31

If we look on Esau's birth-right as only a temporal advantage, what he said had something of truth in it, that our worldly enjoyments, even those we are most fond of, will stand us in no stead in a dying hour. They will not put by the stroke of death, nor ease the pangs, nor remove the sling. But being of a spiritual nature, his undervaluing it, was the greatest profaneness imaginable. It is egregious folly to part with our interest in God, and Christ, and heaven, for the riches, honours, and pleasures of this world. (ENOT)

This was a moment of weakness for Esau. Had he not been famished, this would not have happened. But the moment of weakness was empowered by some underlying thoughts. It is obvious that he valued the open fields and the thrill of the hunt more than tending the herds and flocks of his father. He would rather be out on his own finding wild game than managing assets. Jacob, in contrast, loved being around the herdsmen. He loved staying around the community. He had given careful thought as to what the birthright meant. He valued it. But **Esau despised his birthright** (v. 34). In this moment of weakness, what Esau valued came out. He signed over his birthright to Jacob. Now Jacob would inherit the bulk of Isaac's wealth.

Our attitudes and values show up under pressure. It was when Esau was famished that his attitude about his birthright emerged. We may think that our attitude toward money doesn't matter because we don't have much of it. We might not think that our attitude toward a real experience with God matters. But when the pressure is on, attitudes emerge. Some bad things can happen when the wrong attitudes we hold are combined with stress. In times like these, what is in our hearts is revealed.

Steal the Blessing (Gen. 27:6–10, 30–31, 34–35)

More than the material wealth, Jacob seemed to intuitively grasp what it meant to be blessed. Since he was a boy, he would have heard the stories of his grandfather. He would have been told about the covenant God made with Abraham. He would have heard the stories of how the blessing of God was handed down to Isaac. He would have heard how this blessing was the basis of Isaac finding Rebekah for a wife. He would have heard how, because of the blessing, Isaac's herds multiplied compared to other herds. He would have heard how God walked with his grandfather and spoke to his father and mother. He wanted that blessing in his life.

There was something within Jacob that began when he was small and followed him all through his life. He wanted the blessing of God. When Jacob wrestled the angel (Gen. 32), his demand was for a blessing. Jacob understood the power of the blessing.

> ## WORDS FROM WESLEY
>
> *Genesis 27:6*
>
> Rebekah is here contriving to procure the blessing for Jacob, which was designed for Esau. If the end was good, the means were bad, and no way justifiable. If it were not a wrong to Esau to deprive him of the blessing, he himself having forfeited it by selling the birthright, yet it was a wrong to Isaac, taking advantage of his infirmity, to impose upon him: it was a wrong to Jacob, whom she taught to deceive, by putting a lye in his mouth. If Rebekah, when she heard Isaac promise the blessing to Esau, had gone to him, and with humility and seriousness put him in remembrance of that which God had said concerning their sons; if she had farther shewed him how Esau had forfeited the blessing, both by selling his birth-right, and by marrying of strange wives; 'tis probable Isaac would have been prevailed with to confer the blessing upon Jacob, and needed not thus to have been cheated into it. This had been honourable and laudable, and would have looked well in history; but God left her to herself to take this indirect course, that He might have the glory of bringing good out of evil. (ENOT)

It is one thing to have Esau disavow the birthright with its wealth. But Esau never willingly gave up this blessing. He saw a distinction between the two (Gen. 27:36). Nor was it Isaac's intention to give the blessing to anyone but Esau.

Rebekah, however, wanted Jacob to receive the blessing. So she conspired with Jacob to steal the blessing and the birthright. So now we have a grandfather who lied, a father who lied, and a mother and a son who used deception. We also have a grandfather who was blessed, a father who was blessed, and now a son who wants to be blessed. Both deception and desire for blessing run in the family.

Jacob was unsure of Rebekah's plan, but he joined in with the deception anyway. His issue was not the morality of deception but the consequences of being caught (v. 13). His greatest fear was to get the opposite of a blessing—a curse. But Jacob's desire for blessing outweighed the risks. Jacob, as instructed by his mother, pulled two goats from the flock. Rebekah cooked them, and Jacob took the food to his father. He presented himself as Esau and the food as wild game.

WORDS FROM WESLEY

Genesis 27:6

Father, I joyfully believe
Thou art well-pleased with me;
Thou dost at my approach perceive
An heavenly fragrancy;
Thou dost thy gracious will declare,
Thou dost delight to bless;
And why? My brother's garb I wear,
My Saviour's righteousness. (PW, vol. 9, 26)

Isaac, thinking the son was Esau because of his poor vision (v. 1), blessed Jacob with the blessing of the nations. He also made Jacob to rule over Esau (vv. 28–29). After the blessing was given, Jacob left. Almost immediately, Esau came in from hunting. Esau asked for the blessing. Isaac trembled at the realization the he had blessed Jacob rather than Esau. Isaac told Esau, **"Your brother came deceitfully and took your blessing"** (v. 35).

WORDS FROM WESLEY

Genesis 27:29

Cursed be every one that curseth thee—Let God be a friend to all thy friends, and an enemy to all thine enemies. Now certainly more is comprised in this blessing than appears at first; it must amount to an entail of the promise of the Messiah: that was in the patriarchal dialect the blessing. (ENOT)

Blessings are like words—once spoken, they cannot be taken back. Once given, they cannot be retrieved. Esau's only hope was that there were other blessings left for him (v. 36). Esau's words are very telling: "He has deceived me these two times: He took my birthright, and now he's taken my blessing!" (v. 36).

These stories are messy. Jacob desired what was right, but preyed on his brother in a moment of weakness. He coveted what was good and used deception to get it. The story would be a lot cleaner if we could paint Jacob as good and Esau as bad. But the story isn't told that way. Jacob comes out the winner and Esau the loser. The value that Jacob placed on the birthright and the blessing was the determining factor in this story.

There are some things we can admire yet also detest about Jacob. The Bible never says, "Be like Jacob." The Bible is not promoting deception. Nor is it saying that the end justifies the means. Our call is not to emulate Jacob, but to learn from him. Esau can also teach us some valuable lessons about God and ourselves.

This story of Jacob and Esau would also be far less messy if the blessing of God was explained in a less materialistic way. It would be great if the promise of blessing were love, joy, peace, and happiness. But at this point in the Old Testament, the blessing of God is understood in terms of land, possessions, children, long life, power, and wealth.

We cannot ignore the fact that the blessing of God here in Genesis meant wealth. Nor can we get away from the questions of Jeremiah: "Why does the way of the wicked prosper? Why do all the faithless live at ease?" (Jer. 12:1). And we cannot ignore the questions of Job: "Why do the wicked live on, growing old and increasing in power?" (Job 21:7). Or the complaint of David: "This is what the wicked are like—always carefree, they increase in wealth. Surely in vain have I kept my heart pure; in vain have I washed my hands in innocence" (Ps. 73:12–13).

David's complaint was that the wicked were living the "blessed" life and the pure were downtrodden.

The Bible is meant to be taken as a whole. In our story of Jacob and Esau, the blessing of God means one thing. In other parts of the Old Testament, the blessing of God means something else. In the New Testament, it means something else again. The point of this story is to show that Jacob understood what the blessing of God meant in his context and how he wanted that blessing. The blessing of God is no less valuable in our context.

Most of us live in Esau's world. We say with Esau, "I am a successful hunter because of my skill." Today's version of this is, "I have good children, because I parented right" or "I am a self-made man" or "It has been my hard work that has gotten me what I have." Most of us live in such a way that we are oblivious to the blessings of God. Or we act as if the only blessing that counts is that we are on our way to heaven.

Many times today the only time we ask for the blessing of God is when we bless our food—whatever that means. But the blessing of God was a worthy pursuit for Jacob. His greatest desire was to see God bless him. The blessing of God is still a worthy pursuit.

DISCUSSION

Sibling rivalry seems to flare up occasionally or often in families. Have you observed destructive, long-standing sibling rivalry? The phenomenon isn't new; it blighted Isaac and Rebekah's family.

1. How has sibling rivalry affected your family or a family you know?

2. How might sibling rivalry flare up among brothers and sisters in Christ?

3. How did Esau show a lack of regard for his birthright? How might a believer disrespect his or her spiritual inheritance? Why is spiritual inheritance of greater value than even a cherished family inheritance?

4. Why do you agree or disagree that Esau's physical condition contributed to his disregard for his birthright?

5. How might one's physical condition influence his or her decision-making?

6. How did Rebekah contribute to her children's sibling rivalry? How might a parent properly address the issue of sibling rivalry?

7. How do you interpret the greeting "May the Lord bless you"?

8. Tell why you agree or disagree with the statement "Most of us live in Esau's world."

PRAYER

Lord, help us establish priorities that are honoring to You and consistent with Your Word. Help us get back on track when the circumstances of life beckon us away from those godly priorities.

9

RESOLVING PAINFUL RELATIONSHIPS

Genesis 31:1–3, 26–29, 41–42, 51–55

The reality of conflict underscores the value
of the art of conflict resolution.

On his first attempt to hurl a boomerang, a nine-year-old Australian boy named Max suffered a severe facial injury. His boomerang came back, smacked him in the face, and severed his nose from his cheek. Suffering severe pain, he was rushed to a hospital, where plastic surgery corrected the injury.

Using deception can be as dangerous as an unskilled attempt to hurl a boomerang. It can come back to the deceiver and cause great pain. This study shows how Jacob, the deceiver, became the object of deception at the hand of his uncle. Fortunately, the two deceivers experienced some reconciliation.

COMMENTARY

The book of Genesis divides neatly into four sections: primeval prologue, 1:1—11:26; Abraham cycle, 11:27—25:18; Jacob cycle, 25:19—36:43; and Joseph cycle, 37–50. (Like many things in Old Testament studies, some of these dividing points are debated.) Isaac does not have his own "cycle" because in literary terms he functions as a transitional figure between Abraham and Jacob; no stories are totally about Isaac alone.

With the previous study, we moved from the Abraham cycle to the Jacob cycle. Rebekah found a deceitful way for Jacob, instead of Esau, to receive the blessing of their elderly father, Isaac. Esau vowed revenge, promising that he would kill Jacob after their father died. Rebekah persuaded Isaac to send Jacob north to her father's house in Haran so he could find a wife there among their relatives.

Genesis 28 relates Jacob's dream at Bethel, in which God promised to be with him. Genesis 29 is the story of Jacob's arrival at Haran, his meeting Rachel at the well, and his marriage to Laban's daughters, Leah and Rachel. Here Jacob began to get back as he had given by way of deception, for Laban deceived Jacob into marrying Leah, though he had agreed Jacob's work would earn him the right to marry Rachel. Chapter 30 relates the increase of Jacob's family, then of his wealth, primarily in sheep and goats.

God's Instruction to Jacob (Gen. 31:1–3)

Jacob had worked for Laban fourteen years—seven for Leah, then seven for Rachel. Laban persuaded him to stay on for a wage from the flock. Exactly how (or even whether) Jacob manipulated the genetics of Laban's flocks remains a mystery, but each time Laban changed Jacob's wages in lambs and kids in favor of himself, the offspring were born, instead, to Jacob's advantage.

Even though Jacob had grown rich, Laban by no means had become poor. Yet **Laban's sons** (v. 1) exaggerated their father's losses, as those with a supposed grievance often do. They imagined that if it hadn't been for Jacob, their father would be half again, or twice, as rich in flocks as he now was. Moreover, they took their father's losses as their own, since they were his heirs.

Neither Laban nor his sons took account of the fact, noted several times in these chapters, that Laban had been blessed because of Jacob's presence and involvement with their livestock. Though Jacob now had much, and had started his flocks from Laban's stock, Laban would have had less, not more, had Jacob not been there. But **Jacob noticed that Laban's attitude toward him was not what it had been** (v. 2).

At this point God intervened, telling Jacob to **go back** (v. 3) home to Canaan. For Jacob the crucial reassurance would have been

God's last words here: **"I will be with you."** That had been God's promise on Jacob's outward journey, when God had appeared to him in his dream at Bethel (28:15). Only in that assurance could Jacob find the courage to return and face his brother Esau, whom he had wronged so grievously.

WORDS FROM WESLEY

Genesis 31:3

The Lord said unto Jacob, Return and I will be with thee— Though Jacob had met with very hard usage, yet he would not quit his place 'till God bid him. He came thither by orders from heaven, and there he would stay 'till he was ordered back. The direction he had from heaven is more fully related in the account he gives of it to his wives, where he tells them of the dream he had about the cattle, and the wonderful increase of those of his colour; and how the angel of God in that dream instructed him that it was not by chance, nor by his own policy, that he obtained that great advantage; but by the providence of God, who had taken notice of the hardships Laban had put upon him, and in performance of His promise. (ENOT)

Laban's Grievance against Jacob (Gen. 31:26–29)

Apparently taking advantage of the sheep-shearing season, which was both a hardworking and festive occasion, Jacob sent for his two wives. Leah and Rachel naturally would have brought their entire households out to the fields, the steppelands, in response to Jacob's message (31:4). Thus, all Jacob's family and possessions were ready, so they set out, traveling as fast as small children and many animals would allow them to.

Laban heard (v. 22) and pursued, but did not catch up with Jacob until Jacob was almost home; he had reached Gilead, east of the Jordan and southern Canaan, where Isaac was (v. 23). Though he now had only a few miles to go, Jacob did not actually reach Isaac at Mamre (near the later Hebron) until later (35:27).

What Laban might have done we can only guess, but God appeared to him in a dream and warned him against further manipulation in his dealings with Jacob (31:24). Lest we be too hard on Laban, we should note that **"You've deceived me"** (v. 26) may be a deceptive translation. The clause is, literally, "You have stolen my heart." Since Laban followed that immediately with the accusation **"You've carried off my daughters like captives in war,"** and later lamented not being able to **kiss** his **grandchildren and** his **daughters good-by** (v. 28), we must credit Laban with a measure of paternal feeling.

Yet given Laban's earlier manipulative treatment of Jacob—not once, but many times—and his attitude of animosity that had prompted Jacob to think about leaving, we also must give weight to Laban's next damaging revelation to Jacob. Note the present tense of his declaration: **"I *have* the power to harm you"** (v. 29, emphasis added). If we take Laban's words at face value, the only reason he did not seize everything of Jacob's, and perhaps even kill him, was God's express forbidding in his dream the night before. Certainly, Jacob understood Laban's attitude this way in his own statement: "You would surely have sent me away empty-handed" (v. 42). Jacob also recognized this as an instance of God's fulfilling the promise, "I will be with you" (v. 3), given to him with God's instruction to return home to Canaan and his father.

WORDS FROM WESLEY

Genesis 31:29

It is in the power of my hand to do you hurt—He supposeth that he had both right on his side, and strength on his side, either to revenge the wrong, or recover the right. Yet he owns himself under the restraint of God's power; he durst not injure one of whom he saw to be the particular care of heaven. (ENOT)

Verse 30 reinforces this view of Laban's continuing hostile attitude toward Jacob, as his final accusation had nothing to do with his daughters or grandchildren: "Why did you steal my gods?"

Jacob's Grievance against Laban (Gen. 31:41–42)

Jacob invited Laban to search his camp. Laban did so, but failed to find his "gods," small portable images people worshiped in their homes and carried with them when they traveled. In fact, Rachel had taken them, but her ruse worked when Laban entered her tent to look for them.

Perceiving Laban's charge as a false accusation, Jacob now became angry in his turn, all the years of his frustration since his father-in-law had deceived him with Leah boiling to the surface in his own tirade. **"You changed my wages ten times"** (v. 41); if the first time was Laban's substituting Leah for Rachel on Jacob's first wedding night, Laban still changed Jacob's wages in lambs and kids from the flocks every eight months during the last six years of his management of Laban's livestock. Shepherding contracts usually were written a year at a time. This means Laban did not honor even one of his contracts with Jacob during this period. Jacob the deceiver had been paid back with actions like his own.

Yet in all this, Jacob now recognized God's provision and protection. By itself, Jacob's reference to God as **the God of Abraham and the Fear of Isaac** (v. 42) could be taken as distancing himself from God. But these honorific titles for God do not stand alone in Jacob's speech. He recognized that God had been with him also, as God had been with his grandfather and his father. God was fulfilling the promise made at Bethel.

The title **the Fear of Isaac** does not use the common Hebrew word for fear or reverence. Some translate here the "Kinsman" or the "Refuge" of Isaac.

WORDS FROM WESLEY

Genesis 31:42

Jacob speaks of God as the God of his father, intimating that he thought himself unworthy to be thus regarded, but was beloved for his father's sake. He calls him the God of Abraham and the fear of Isaac: for Abraham was dead, and gone to that world where there is no fear; but Isaac was yet alive, sanctifying the Lord in his heart as his fear and his dread. (ENOT)

The Uneasy Reconciliation of Jacob and Laban (Gen. 31:51–55)

Laban recognized he was beaten, or at least he was afraid to challenge God's command in his dream. So he proposed they "make a covenant" (v. 44), a sacrificial ceremony binding both parties to fulfill completely all the terms of their agreement, under threat of death, as they had killed the animals for the covenantal sacrifice.

Jacob agreed and organized the building of two stone memorials to the occasion. The first was a standing stone pillar, the second a pile of stones gathered into a single heap (vv. 45–46). Laban's final recorded words are recognition of the function of these two monuments as fixed, silent witnesses to their covenant agreement. Genesis 31:51–52 reads like an excerpt from a written legal document. Though the text does not mention it, it would have been customary to execute and sign written copies of such a covenant agreement, probably on clay tablets, one for each man.

Laban probably had intended Jacob **harm** (v. 52), at least the harm of robbing him of all he had acquired—else why pursue Jacob at all? Now, under God's prior constraint, he pledged not to **go past this heap** to harm Jacob in any way. But Laban did not trust the man he had victimized repeatedly not to retaliate if the opportunity arose. This is clear from his invoking the names of Jacob's grandfather Abraham, his own grandfather Nahor, and their common great-grandfather Terah (the latter not by name) as titles of God, as he called on God to be the guarantor of his own and Jacob's good faith (v. 53). This, even though Laban apparently did not himself worship this God, the God of his grandfather, his great-grandfather, and his great-uncle!

All this talk and activity led up to one thing: reconciliation between Laban and Jacob. But that this reconciliation was, or became, genuine—even though perhaps still grudging on Laban's part—is indicated in language it would be easy for the Westerner to miss: Jacob **offered a sacrifice . . . and invited his relatives to a meal** (v. 54). Whether this was the same sacrifice and meal referred to in verses 44–46 is not entirely clear, though it seems more likely than not.

In either case, eating a meal together was the climactic, sacred, and clinching act, as important as their agreeing together on the terms of the covenant, and Jacob's setting up of the two stone memorials. Laban could not sit as Jacob's guest and partake of his lavish hospitality on such a high occasion then turn around later and attack him in any way, directly or indirectly. It would have been an unspeakably dishonorable act, shaming him and his sons for generations. However difficult it had been to arrive at, and whether embraced in feeling wholeheartedly or not, this was a genuine reconciliation. Both Laban and Jacob could rest easy, each knowing he now had nothing to fear from the other.

WORDS FROM WESLEY

Genesis 31:54

And Jacob sware by the fear of his father Isaac—The God whom his father Isaac feared, who had never served other gods, as Abraham and Nahor had done. (ENOT)

Laban rose **early the next morning** (v. 55) and did what he had professed previously to have missed so badly; he **kissed his grandchildren and his daughters and blessed them**. Though Laban ended his part in the biblical drama as a man difficult to admire, we may respect his heavyhearted sadness as he rode away from the daughters and grandchildren he never would see again and forever out of the pages of sacred history.

Many places later in Scripture, we are advised and encouraged to make every effort to accomplish reconciliation with those we have wronged or who have wronged us. Though a sad figure heading home, Laban still is a concrete example of the rightness and goodness of that instruction. At least Laban went away not still embittered, but reconciled, with his loved ones. In the ensuing years, Laban, Jacob, Leah, and Rachel would have had that comforting memory to fall back on.

DISCUSSION

Occasionally, relatives become so resentful of each other that they choose to live far apart to avoid seeing each other. This study relates the story of reunion between a man and his father-in-law.

1. What poetic justice, if any, do you see in the fact that Jacob worked for tricky Laban for fourteen years? Why do you agree or disagree that the Lord had orchestrated this relationship for Jacob's good?

2. How did Jacob know the time was right for him to go back home?

3. Read James 4:13–15. Why is it so important to follow the Lord's will in every decision-making process?

4. Read Genesis 31:22–25. Why do you agree or disagree that Jacob's life was in jeopardy?

5. Read Genesis 31:49. Do you think Laban's words should be exchanged between believers as a token of mutual love? Why or why not?

6. How might estranged family members heal their broken relationship?

7. Why is it important in a congregation to mend broken relationships?

8. How do you feel about Laban after reading about his farewell meeting with his daughters and grandchildren?

PRAYER

Lord, give us wisdom to trust the trustworthy and to keep at bay those who would violate our trust. Of course, make us wholly trustworthy in Your eyes.

10

VICTORY THROUGH STRUGGLE

Genesis 32:9–12, 22–31

God engages us to change us.

A peach grower complained to his pastor that an early, heavy frost had ruined his crop. "Why would God allow that to happen?" the distraught peach grower asked.

"Well," responded the pastor, "perhaps God is more interested in growing you than He is in growing peaches."

Calamities often drive us to desperation, and in our desperation we cry out to God, and then He affects positive change in us. Prayer changes not only things, but also people.

This study shows how a desperate Jacob wrestled in prayer with God and how God subdued his will and made him a better man.

COMMENTARY

Thomas Wolfe once said, "You can't go home again." But that isn't true, especially if God is leading you there! After twenty years in Haran, Jacob had a word from God that instructed him to return home to Canaan (Gen. 31:10–13). Jacob probably didn't realize what an exciting trip this would turn out to be.

Jacob set out from Paddan Aram with his family and all his acquisitions. He crossed the Euphrates River and turned toward the country of Gilead (vv. 17–21). However, his uncle Laban followed him, and it was at Mizpah that Jacob finally made peace with Laban after many years of deceit and deception between them (vv. 25–55).

As Jacob continued his journey, he met angels of God (32:1). Angels were not a new phenomenon to Jacob. He had seen angels at Bethel twenty years before (28:10–12). He declared this to be "God's camp" and named the place Mahanaim, which means "two camps" or "two companies."

Jacob knew he was approaching Seir in Edom, which was where his brother Esau lived. He was fearful of his reunion with his brother; twenty years before, Esau had threatened to kill Jacob for cheating him out of Isaac's blessing (27:41). Instead of trusting God, Jacob gave in to his fears. He sent messengers to go before him to approach Esau and "soften" him up. Through this message, he called himself the "servant" of Esau and tried to impress his brother with his acquired wealth.

But by the time Jacob reached the Jabbok River, the messengers returned to Jacob with the distressing message that Esau was coming to meet Jacob accompanied by four hundred men (32:6). Jacob feared the worst—that Esau was coming to fulfill his threat of twenty years ago to take his life. This fear gripped Jacob's heart, and so he divided his camp into two. His strategy was that if Esau attacked one, the other camp would be able to escape.

Jacob's fear and guilty conscience were controlling him. Instead of remembering the vision of the angels God had sent to assure him that he was safe, Jacob allowed his fear to overtake him and, therefore, he reverted back to his old scheming ways. At this point, Jacob realized that only God could save him, and so he went to the Lord in prayer. Because of this, we have one of the greatest prayers recorded in Scripture.

God doesn't want us to just live keeping the status quo. He is in the business of changing us. This can only happen when we come to the end of ourselves. This was the case in Jacob's life. He had lived his life relying on his own wits. But God was bringing him home to make some permanent changes in Jacob. He wants to make those same changes in us as well.

Jacob Prayed (Gen. 32:9–12)

The content of this prayer reveals that Jacob had a great understanding of God, yet he lacked the ability to transfer these truths into personal living. Praying in desperation, he appealed to God to deliver him.

He began his prayer by addressing God as the God of Abraham and Isaac (v. 9). He knew about how his father and grandfather had entered into a covenant relationship with God. They had shared their personal experiences with him. Jacob knew that God was a God of grace because of his family history. But knowing about the relationship others have with God is not sufficient. God had confirmed His covenant with Jacob at Bethel some twenty years before. But Jacob had not yet realized what that meant to him personally. We cannot live off someone else's relationship with the Lord. We must learn to appropriate God's promises to our lives individually. Jacob was still learning to do this.

He then reminded the Lord that it was not his idea to return home to Canaan (v. 9). God instructed him to do so while he was still in Paddan Aram (31:13). This was the fulfillment of what God promised him at Bethel (28:15).

But Jacob did not realize that God does not ask anything of us without first enabling us to do what He has asked. So often when we feel God is leading us, we believe everything should go smoothly—that there should be no bumps in the road. God isn't interested in making things easy for us, but in transforming us into the image of His Son, Jesus Christ. God was using this situation to cause Jacob to rely totally on Him rather than his old scheming ways.

Jacob also prayed back to God His promise to **make you prosper** (32:9). When we think of prosperity, we usually think of material gain. God had already fulfilled this promise. Jacob was returning home with a large family and great possessions.

However, this Hebrew word has a greater meaning. It literally means "to make well." God was promising that He would cause Jacob not only to be successful and happy in his endeavors, but He would also make his life pleasing to God. And when we get right down to it, pleasing God is the true measure of success.

Jacob also recognized how God had blessed him, even though he did not deserve any of it (v. 10). Jacob fled to Paddan Aram with nothing more than the clothes on his back, but his family had become large enough to divide into two groups. It is important that we take time to meditate on God's goodness to us even though we are not worthy of such blessings. Sometimes we begin to think that God "owes" us His blessing. Jacob had stolen the blessing from his brother Esau, but now he was realizing that all he had was a gift of God; nothing had come through his own efforts.

He then asked God to save him from his brother Esau. He admitted his own fear: **"I am afraid he will come and attack me"** (v. 11). Facing our fears is an important part of God's transforming process. As long as we are in denial, God cannot work in our lives. But when we are willing to admit our fears, the door begins to open to trusting God.

Jacob then reminded God of still another promise to him: **"I will . . . make your descendants like the sand of the sea, which cannot be counted"** (v. 12). Jacob was trying to understand how this promise could be fulfilled if Esau would be allowed to destroy him and his family. How could God's eternal plan be destroyed by one angry man? Whatever God promises, He will do, even when circumstances seem to indicate otherwise. It is in times like these that our faith in Him is tested and strengthened.

Jacob's prayer can be a model for us. We need to understand that we are not entitled to God's favor. We must rely on God's very nature or character and not our own ability. And we must be honest about our fears and doubts and express them to God.

When we do this, God is able to work in our lives beyond what we can even imagine.

WORDS FROM WESLEY
Genesis 32:12

Thou saidst, I will surely do thee good—The best we can say to God in prayer is, what He hath said to us. God's promises as they are the surest guide of our desires in prayer, and furnish us with the best petitions, so they are the firmest ground of our hopes, and furnish us with the best pleas. *Thou saidst, I will do thee good*—Lord, do me good in this matter. He pleads also a particular promise, that of the multiplying of his seed. Lord, what will become of that promise, if they be all cut off? (ENOT)

Jacob Wrestled (Gen. 32:22–26)

Still concerned for his own safety, Jacob sent his wives and family on ahead of him. Behind them, he sent his possessions (v. 22). At this point, Jacob was completely alone (v. 24). Likewise, when we are totally alone, not relying on anyone or anything, God can do something new in our lives. This was the case in Jacob's life.

Scripture tells us that **a man wrestled with him till daybreak** (v. 24). We are not told exactly who this man was. Some claim this was a theophany, a pre-incarnate appearance of Jesus Christ. Others say he was an angelic being. His identity is not entirely clear. But we do know that this wrestling match certainly symbolized Jacob's struggle with God in order to obtain His blessing. This was not a momentary struggle, but one that lasted until dawn. Being serious about receiving all God has for our lives is not an emotional whim, but an experience that takes all of our strength. How serious are you about receiving all God desires to give you?

The man saw that he was not able to overpower Jacob (v. 25). This does not mean Jacob was stronger than God. It means he was not willing to give up. For Jacob said, **"I will not let you go unless**

you bless me" (v. 26). The blessing of God had been important to Jacob from the very beginning. He had connived in order to receive the blessing of the firstborn from his father. And now he was struggling to receive a blessing from his heavenly Father's hand.

WORDS FROM WESLEY

Genesis 32:24

Very early in the morning, a great while before day. Jacob had helped his wives and children over the river, and he desired to be private, and was left alone, that he might again spread his cares and fears before God in prayer. While Jacob was earnest in prayer, stirring up himself to take hold on God, an angel takes hold on him. Some think this was a created angel, one of those that always behold the face of our Father. Rather it was the angel of the covenant, who often appeared in a human shape, before he assumed the human nature. We are told by the prophet, Hos. 12:4 how Jacob wrestled, he wept and made supplication; prayers and tears were his weapons. It was not only a corporal, but a spiritual wrestling by vigorous faith and holy desire. (ENOT)

In the struggle, the man touched Jacob's hip. Some commentators believe the hip was dislocated. Others believe a ligament was torn. Whatever the case, Jacob was left with a limp. Some have called this the "wound of grace"—a reminder of God's great mercy toward Jacob.

WORDS FROM WESLEY

Genesis 32:36

And he said, I will not let thee go except them bless me—He resolves he will have a blessing, and rather shall all his bones be put out of joint, than he will go away without one. Those that would have the blessing of Christ must be in good earnest, and be importunate for it. (ENOT)

A. W. Tozer is noted as having said, "The Lord cannot fully bless a man until He has first conquered him." This is exactly what happened to Jacob. God conquered Jacob and his deceptive heart. A transformation was in process.

Jacob Was Changed (Gen. 32:27–31)

The man then asked Jacob, **"What is your name?"** (v. 27). This was not because God needed to know who Jacob was, but because He wanted Jacob to examine himself. Today, names are given because we like the way they sound. In Bible times, names represented the person to whom they were given and were often prophetic of what would happen in that person's life. In responding, Jacob was reminded that his name means "heel catcher" or "supplanter" or "deceiver." That had been exactly what Jacob's life was to this point.

In asking him his name, God was also giving Jacob a second chance. When Jacob stole Esau's blessing, Isaac asked this same question: "Who are you, my son?" Jacob lied and said he was Esau (Gen. 27:18–19). Now God was giving him an opportunity to own up to who he was. In responding that his name was Jacob, he was confessing that he had been a deceiver. But he was not to remain as one.

God changed Jacob's name. **"Your name will no longer be Jacob, but Israel, because you have struggled with God and with men and have overcome"** (v. 28). The name **Israel** comes from a Hebrew word that means "to struggle." Some translate it as "God strives" or "let God rule." Jacob had lost the wrestling match but won God's blessing.

Jacob moved from being self-mastered to coming under the full authority and control of God himself. Jacob was now able to be trusted with God's authority, which would eventually be transferred to his sons, who one day became a nation. It is interesting to note that God's chosen people are called Israel even to this day. God is looking for people who will allow Him to master them and to rule their lives.

Jacob realized that this was a life-changing event. And so he changed the name of this place to **Peniel** (v. 30), which means "the face of God" because **"I saw God face to face, and yet my life was spared."** He had believed that seeing God's face would bring him death, but in actuality it brought him life. Jacob left Peniel a changed man. He had a new heart, a new name, a new walk (with a limp), and a new relationship with God. God wants to do the same for us.

WORDS FROM WESLEY
Genesis 32:31

He halted on his thigh—And some think he continued to do so to his dying day. If he did, he had no reason to complain, for the honour and comfort he obtained by his struggle was abundantly sufficient to countervail the damage, though he went limping to his grave. (ENOT)

A popular worship song a few years ago said, "I'm desperate for You." The question each one of us needs to ask ourselves is how desperate are we for God? Are we willing to wrestle with the Lord in prayer until we too are transformed into the very nature of God in a real and practical way? God wants to work in you. Are you willing to let Him have His way?

DISCUSSION

Share if you pray fervently when you find yourself in a desperate situation. If you do, you can relate to Jacob. Knowing Esau was approaching with an armed contingent, Jacob wrestled in prayer with God until daybreak.

1. What do you learn from Genesis 32:10 about Jacob's attitude toward himself and God?

2. Do you agree or disagree that humility is a prerequisite to answered prayer?

3. According to Genesis 32:11, Jacob's prayer was specific. Do you think your prayers are often too general? Why or why not?

4. What specific request(s) do you need to present to God today?

5. How is Jacob's prayer a model for us?

6. Why do you agree or disagree that we need to offer lengthy prayers if we want God to hear us?

7. Why do you agree or disagree that God is more interested in hearing us pray than we are in praying?

8. How has prayer changed you?

PRAYER

Lord, may we never forget how far You have brought us. Remind us of the ways You have been faithful to us in the past that we may increase our confidence in You for the challenges we'll face in the future.

11

TRACING GOD'S HAND, TRUSTING GOD'S HEART

Genesis 37:2–11; 45:4–9

God works through people to accomplish His purposes.

A TV comedy featured two brothers who sang, played guitars, and exchanged verbal jabs. One often told his brother, "Mom always liked you best."

We might excuse his poor grammar (he should have said "better"), but we can empathize with his perceived situation. After all, we have all seen family situations in which one or both parents favored one child over another. Such favoritism can produce hurt feelings, spark animosity, and even lead to violence.

This study uncovers Jacob's favoritism of his son Joseph and shows how it stirred Joseph's brothers to hatred and violence. It also shows how God can use even the worst circumstances to accomplish good in a believer's life.

COMMENTARY

We see the baton passed to a new generation, the twelve sons of Jacob, with the focus almost exclusively on Joseph, Jacob's favorite son. The fourth "cycle" of Genesis, the Joseph cycle, begins with the first verse of our first study passage. With the exception of Genesis 38, the rest of the book is about Joseph in terms of the human characters.

Joseph was Jacob's eleventh son, but the first child of his mother, Rachel, Jacob's favorite wife. Indeed, Jacob loved Rachel first and best, and would have married only her had Laban not deceived him on the night of his first marriage and given him Leah instead. Leah bore Jacob six sons and a daughter, and both of the women's maidservants, Bilhah and Zilpah, bore him two sons before Rachel finally bore Joseph.

As though that were not enough, Rachel died giving birth to Joseph's younger brother, Benjamin, leaving the two boys as Jacob's only flesh-and-blood reminder of their mother, whom he had loved from the day he first saw her coming across the field toward him outside Haran.

Since Jacob's encounter at Peniel (Gen. 32), he had met and reconciled with his brother, Esau (Gen. 33). Simeon and Levi had avenged (as they thought) the dishonoring of their full sister Dinah by slaughtering all the men of the city of Shechem, a grossly disproportionate response (Gen. 34). Jacob had met with God again at Bethel; Rachel had died giving birth to Benjamin at Ephrath, a few miles north of Jerusalem; Isaac had died at Mamre (Gen. 35). Genesis 36 is concerned with Esau's descendents.

Jacob's Favoritism (Gen. 37:2–4)

This is the account of Jacob (v. 2): The last of ten such notices in Genesis, referring to family records that were the sources of the information in Genesis to this point. This one closes the Jacob cycle.

Joseph . . . was tending the flocks (v. 2). A good rule of thumb, especially when people already don't like you, is don't rock the boat. Joseph violated that common-sense guideline and tattled to his father about something his half-brothers had done while they were out together with the sheep and goats. Since their offense is not reported and the text says nothing about Jacob's response, we can only guess whether it was a trifling or a serious matter. Whatever their act, Joseph's tattling about it fueled his brothers' growing animosity toward him.

Rather than making an effort to treat his sons equally despite his partiality toward Joseph, Jacob flaunted it by giving Joseph a robe like none of his brothers'. Traditionally, this has been taken as a "coat of many colors." The Hebrew phrase does not necessarily refer to the color of this robe or tunic, but clearly indicates an exceptionally fine garment. Whatever the emotional climate before, Jacob's favoritism became obvious and undeniable to everyone, an irritation to his brothers every time Joseph wore their father's gift to him (v. 4). No doubt, too, he wore it often.

Joseph's Dreams (Gen. 37:5–11)

Joseph could not help having these dreams; indeed, they appear to have come from God. But he could have refrained from revealing his dreams to his brothers and adding fuel to the fire of his brothers' hatred (v. 5).

WORDS FROM WESLEY

Genesis 37:5

Though he was now very young, about seventeen years old, yet he was pious and devout, and this fitted him for God's gracious discoveries to him. Joseph had a great deal of trouble before him, and therefore God gave him betimes this prospect of his advancement, to support and comfort him. (ENOT)

The meaning of Joseph's first dream was clear; as their sheaves in his dream had bowed down to his standing sheaf (vv. 6–7), so his brothers would bow down to Joseph. Joseph's brothers interpreted his dream as an expression of Joseph's desires, and they reacted strongly. One indicator is the repetition of their incredulous question with two different verbs—**reign** and **rule**. **Dream** (v. 8) is plural in the Hebrew text. Apparently, this dream occurred to Joseph more than once. If so, he would have thought the probability of its fulfillment to be greater than if he had dreamed it only once.

●

WORDS FROM WESLEY

Genesis 37:8

The reign of Jesus Christ, our Joseph is despised, and striven against by an unbelieving world, who cannot endure to think that this man should reign over them. (ENOT)

Joseph's second dream was like the first in its import, though its symbolism was different and much grander. **The sun and moon and eleven stars** (v. 9) could mean only one thing, since Joseph had eleven brothers, counting his little brother Benjamin. This time, Jacob **rebuked** Joseph (v. 10); the syntax of his question is the same, and equally as powerful, as that of the brothers' questioning of Joseph's earlier dream. **Your mother** must refer to Leah, since Rachel had died when Joseph was very young.

His father kept the matter in mind (v. 11), much as Mary, centuries later, "treasured up all these things and pondered them in her heart" (Luke 2:19).

Joseph's Dreams Realized (Gen. 45:4–9)

The jealousy of his brothers (37:11) led them to sell Joseph to passing caravanners, who carried him to Egypt. Through a series of adventures that both built and tested Joseph's character, he became chief minister to Pharaoh, in charge of everything that happened in Egypt, answerable only to Pharaoh himself. Having predicted years of famine, he organized the storage of grain beforehand. When the crops failed, Egypt was ready and became the granary for nearby lands as well.

Hit hard by the famine in Canaan, Jacob sent his sons to Egypt to buy grain. Joseph recognized them at once when they came before him and organized a series of tests to see whether they had changed, as he had. Satisfied they had, at the end of their second journey to Egypt, Joseph revealed himself to them as their brother. His dreams had come to pass; they had bowed down to him, not once but several times already.

Joseph did not gloat, but took the high road of forgiveness and recognition of God's providential leading. However, Joseph first had to exercise his absolute authority, because his brothers were too terrified to answer his question, whether their father Jacob still lived (45:3).

The one you sold (v. 4) brought the matter into the open before them all. They had done a heinous act of treachery against their brother, an act that never could be undone. They had done it coldly, callously, and cruelly. Joseph probably could still hear their mocking laughter those many years ago as he pled with them to reconsider: "Where's your ruling over us now, little brother?"

But human vengeance keeps everyone, perpetrator and victim alike, trapped in the past. The only positive way out is forward, and Joseph immediately assured his brothers that he had moved beyond any previous thoughts of revenge. **Do not be distressed** (v. 5); "do not worry that I am going to revenge myself on you— I won't." **Do not be angry with yourselves**; "do not kick yourselves for making a stupid and evil decision that looks now as though it has come back to bite you—it won't."

Because . . . God sent me ahead of you. Wesleyans believe God has foreknowledge of everything that can be known, but not that God preordains human choices and actions. God's interactions with humans may be described as partnering together with us as we choose to partner with God, sometimes working "around" us or in spite of us if we choose to resist God and His good intentions for us and for the rest of His creation.

God worked in and through Joseph's early unwise and immature actions—without directing him to do and say them. God used the exceedingly sinful act of Joseph's brothers in selling him into Egypt—without predestining them to do it. God worked in Joseph's life, in spite of the sexual advances and betrayal of

Potiphar's wife, to put Joseph in position to be the savior of all Egypt and his entire family—without decreeing what she (or Joseph) must do.

Joseph now divulged to his brothers what God had revealed to him through Pharaoh's two dreams almost a decade earlier (Gen. 41); the famine would continue through **the next five years** (45:6). In ancient Egypt, the **plowing** was not done until the annual Nile flood had receded. If the Nile did not flood (the most common cause of famine in Egypt), there was no receding; if no receding, no plowing.

At the very end of verse 5 and again at the very beginning of verse 7, Joseph asserted, **"God sent me ahead of you."** Just as wise, loving, and skilled parents can work both with and in spite of their children for theirs and the family's good, so God worked both with and in spite of the choices of Jacob's dysfunctional family, bringing them down to Egypt, **to preserve . . . and to save** them (v. 7).

Clearly, Joseph's brothers had sold him; God had not predestined them to this evil act; they had done it on their own. At the same time, in the luxury of the panoramic view of hindsight, it was just as correct for Joseph to say **"It was not you . . . but God"** (v. 8).

He made me (v. 8) is literally, "He has placed me." **Father to Pharaoh** (v. 8) refers to Joseph being Pharaoh's most reliable counselor and, in this case, the enabler and preserver of his kingship. Without Joseph, Pharaoh would have lost his throne; Egypt itself may have suffered irreversible losses, becoming but an unrecognizable shadow of its former self.

Father . . . lord . . . and ruler (v. 8) all vividly emphasized that Joseph's dreams had become reality; they had been, in fact, predictions from God. His brothers were under his authority. Now he could, and did, give them a direct order: **"Now hurry back to my father"** (v. 9). Did Joseph say *my* **father** (emphasis added) to remind his brothers they had not acted as loyal sons to Jacob when they sold his favorite son then pretended he had been killed by a wild beast? If so, it was no more than they deserved, and Joseph may have discerned that while the brothers had come a long way from that day, they still had a way to go in their ethical and relational restoration.

WORDS FROM WESLEY

Genesis 45:8

See what a favourable colour he puts upon the injury they had done him. *God sent me before you*—God's Israel is the particular care of God's providence. Joseph reckoned that his advancement was not so much designed to save a whole kingdom of Egyptians, as to preserve a small family of Israelites; for the Lord's portion is His people: whatever goes with others, they shall be secured. How admirable are the projects of Providence! (ENOT)

Joseph even had authority to command his father, **"Come down to me; don't delay"** (v. 9). In this period, Canaan was under Egyptian military and political control. Earlier, answering Joseph's accusation that they were spies, the ten brothers who had come to Egypt the first time protested (42:11) they were not spies, but "loyal men" (not, as often translated, "honest men," which makes no sense in the context).

As Joseph's story vividly illustrates, God works with (if possible) or against (as necessary) the choices of individuals and of nations to accomplish God's eternal and overarching purposes. We are invited into God's good designs and God's loving, joyful family. Our choices cannot thwart God's overall designs, but our final choice determines whether we enjoy what God designed and intended for us or whether, instead, we spend eternity without God, knowing forever it was our own choice, and our choice alone.

DISCUSSION

Everyone dreams, but do those dreams come from God? Jacob's son Joseph had highly unusual dreams that must have come from God. This study traces Joseph's dreams from inception to fulfillment.

1. Why do you agree or disagree that Jacob should have known that favoring one child over the others would cause trouble?

2. Why do you agree or disagree that young Joseph was what might be called a "spoiled brat"?

3. How might parents avoid spoiling a child?

4. What is your opinion of the popular advice "Follow your dreams"? Defend your answer.

5. What kinds of bad behavior have you seen jealousy produce? How can you avoid being jealous of others?

6. How would you apply Romans 8:28 to the events that occurred in Joseph's life?

7. Read John 1:11. What similarity do you see between the treatment Joseph received from his brothers and the treatment Jesus received from His brethren, the Jews?

8. Read Genesis 45:4–9. What purpose was served by Joseph's presence in Egypt?

9. How can a believer make sense of his or her trials?

PRAYER

Lord, give us the courage to grieve the significant losses in our lives so that we might be able to forgive those who caused them.

12

HOW TO BE SUCCESSFUL

Genesis 39:2–6, 11–12, 20–23

What looks like failure in human eyes may
be success in the eyes of God.

Advice often given to kids threatened by bullies is to just walk away. It is good advice for God's people, too, when they face temptation. The apostle Paul advised Timothy, a young pastor, to "flee the evil desires of youth" (2 Tim. 2:22).

Who can deny that temptations abound today? Solicitations to do evil come from the print and electronic media, the entertainment industry, other people, and even from our own lusts. It is important, therefore, that we walk away from temptation, or better yet, to run away.

This study presents Joseph as an example of someone who fled temptation, was falsely accused of attempted rape, and imprisoned. Through it all, he was a success in God's eyes.

COMMENTARY

In the context of these studies, we are approaching the end of our study in selected passages from Genesis. In the previous study, we looked at Joseph's dreams of preeminence among his brothers as a young man (37:2–10), then moved ahead to Joseph's first statement to his brothers upon revealing his identity to them (45:4–9). By then, Joseph had known for some time that God had been the author of his youthful dreams and that God had brought those dreams to reality.

Here, we move back in Joseph's life to his first years in Egypt. The episodes we consider will reveal themselves as formative of

Joseph's mature character and of the deepening of his reliance upon God through very disheartening circumstances.

In the context of the book, we find ourselves still early in the Joseph cycle, Genesis 37:2—50:26. By the end of chapter 37, Joseph had been brought to Egypt and sold to Potiphar, the captain of Pharaoh's guard (37:36). Chapter 38 then breaks away from Joseph to record the story of Judah and Tamar back in Canaan, before returning to Joseph's story in chapter 39.

God's Blessing on Joseph in Potiphar's Household (Gen. 39:2–6)

Four statements about Joseph stand out in this paragraph, statements that can be instructive for anyone whose aim is to live a life both pleasing to God and of appropriate service to others.

The first is that **the LORD was with Joseph** (v. 2). In one sense, God is with everyone because God is everywhere; the theological term is "omnipresent." But God was with Joseph in a deeper sense than that. Joseph became aware of God's presence and came to understand that God desired his company. God's presence is His best gift to us. Difficult as it for us to fathom, it is a gift to God, as well. It appears Joseph learned this early in his Egyptian sojourn.

WORDS FROM WESLEY

Genesis 39:2

Those that can separate us from all our friends, cannot deprive us of the gracious presence of our God. When Joseph had none of his relations with him, he had his God with him, even in the house of the Egyptian: Joseph was banished from his father's house, but the Lord was with him. It is God's presence with us that makes all we do prosperous. Those that would prosper, must therefore make God their friend; and those that do prosper, must therefore give God the praise. (ENOT)

It should not be surprising, then, that Joseph **prospered** (Hebrew, "And he was a man of success"; v. 2). The key is to understand what God means by success. We will see several dimensions of "success" as we proceed, but here in this opening paragraph of Joseph's story in Egypt, we see what many people assume success to be. **The LORD gave him success in everything he did** (v. 3); when all our projects work out spectacularly well, we are prone to conclude God is blessing us. Often, that is true, but never is it the whole truth.

The second statement about Joseph is that he **found favor** (v. 4) in Potiphar's eyes; that is, Potiphar looked on him with favor and treated him favorably. Thus, Joseph experienced another dimension of success that is part of many people's definition of the term. Again, this often is a part of success, but never is it the whole; having the right connections is not all it takes to be "successful" by God's definition.

Third, Potiphar **entrusted to** Joseph's **care everything he owned** (v. 4). This statement is repeated in verse 6, with the further astounding declaration that Potiphar **did not concern himself with anything except the food he ate**.

Now we're getting closer to understanding how God defines success. Doing things "successfully" and being an attractive personality can happen with a combination of circumstances and skills that may or may not reflect anything of character. Earning trust usually requires character and the time for others to discover it in one. (Even those who breach trust usually have earned it legitimately at first, then have strayed from the path of integrity.)

Finally, God blessed others because of Joseph; verse 5 says it twice so we're sure not to miss it. Potiphar and his entire household were blessed specifically because of Joseph's presence and oversight. Incidentally, the final phrases of verse 5, **in the house and in the field**, reveal a glimpse into the scale of ancient Egyptian life. Potiphar was chief of Pharaoh's guard, yet he also possessed fields and, therefore, livestock; their mention here is very much matter-of-fact, as though that were normal, which it was. In that respect, ancient Egypt was more like feudal Europe in medieval times than our own time.

God's blessing on others because of the presence and efforts of God's people is an important element of God's definition, often missing in our garden-variety thinking about success. Success is not only, or even primarily, the enlarging of our own assets; after all, in this phase of his life, Joseph had nothing he could call his own.

Verses 5–6 further emphasize these elements of Joseph's success, by God's definition of success, by the use of the literary device of *chiasm* (KY-asm), named for the Greek letter *chi*, which looks like English X. A given number of elements occur, then are reversed—crossed over like an X—so the first and last are the same, and the middle two are the same. This chiasm is very simple: (a) Potiphar trusted Joseph (v. 5); (b) God blessed Potiphar (v. 5); (b') God blessed Potiphar (v. 5); (a') Potiphar continued to trust Joseph (v. 6).

Now Joseph was well-built and handsome (v. 6); Joseph came by his build and good looks honestly. Genesis 29:17 uses exactly the same phrase to describe Rachel, Joseph's mother, when his father, Jacob, first had met her.

WORDS FROM WESLEY

Genesis 39:6

When she laid hold on him, he *left his garment in her hand*—He would not stay to parley with the temptation, but flew out from it with the utmost abhorrence, he left his garment as one escaping for his life. (ENOT)

Of course, this is not just a gratuitous observation. It sets up the aggressive action of Potiphar's wife, over a long period of time, to try to seduce Joseph. She found him attractive, as did almost everyone else.

Joseph's Resolute Act to Keep Faith with God and Potiphar (Gen. 39:11–12)

Verses 8–10 spell out that Potiphar's wife was very persistent over a long period of time in trying to persuade Joseph to sleep with her. Equally, Joseph displayed solid moral understanding in his steadfast refusal of her advances. It would be a betrayal of her husband, who had entrusted everyone and everything else in his household to Joseph's complete oversight and control, except her (vv. 8–9). Even more importantly, Joseph viewed such a breach as "sin against God" (v. 9). Both God's glory and our well-being are best served when we maintain integrity in all our relationships, both with God and with other people. To fail is to sin against God, others, and ourselves.

"Or even be with her" (v. 10) is evidence of Joseph's continual watchful prudence. But there came a day when he went into the house and no other man was inside. The Hebrew text is quite specific in saying, "There was none of the men of the house there within" (39:11 KJV). In light of this statement, perhaps Joseph thought another manservant was, or would be, in the house, but he found out, too late, none were present. Certainly, one or more of the women servants were in the house, in attendance upon Potiphar's wife or involved in other household tasks, but she easily controlled them, out of loyalty or fear, or both.

She caught him by his cloak (v. 12); the Hebrew is the more general "by his clothing." Given Egypt's warm climate, we should envision an outer garment, a bit on the heavier side if this happened during the winter, lighter if it was another time of year.

Potiphar's wife was not to be put off at this best opportunity in a long time, or so she thought. How could this foreign slave refuse the mistress of the house when she insisted so strongly as to lay hands on him?

But Joseph did refuse, putting into action the conviction he had expressed earlier (vv. 8–9). The verbs suggest quick, reflexive action without thought—Joseph had thought this through already— and with no attempt to reason with her. Joseph did perhaps all he could have thought to do, and his actions are helpful models for anyone faced with temptation or struggling to remove oneself from the grip of sin already indulged in. From the time of the woman's first advances, Joseph had done his best to avoid situations where the mistress of the household would have the opportunity to proposition him again.

Joseph was right, too, not to grab or strike his master's wife, even though she had grasped his clothing. However unfairly, that would have been a real offense against her, and he could not have defended himself when she charged him with it. At least he was exonerated, eventually, of her false charge of attempted rape. In the interim, however, Potiphar believed his wife's version of events, and threw Joseph into prison.

God's Blessing on Joseph in the Royal Prison (Gen. 39:20–23)

We already know Potiphar was Pharaoh's captain of the guard (37:36; 39:1). Thus, it is no surprise he could put Joseph in **the place where the king's prisoners were confined** (v. 20). This detail is mentioned here, however, because it will be important for the reader to know as Joseph's story develops.

We would understand if we were to read that Joseph wondered how much more "success" God intended to bless him with! His sexual integrity had landed him in prison for attempted rape. From the tone of this account, however, we should conclude that if Joseph did discuss with God the unfairness of it all, he also understood **the LORD was with him** (v. 21) even in the prison and trusted God to vindicate him in God's timing.

WORDS FROM WESLEY
Genesis 39:20

Where the king's prisoners were bound—Potiphar, it is likely, chose that prison because it was the worst; for there the irons entered into the soul, Psalm 105:18 but God designed it to pave the way to His enlargement. Our Lord Jesus, like Joseph was bound, and numbered with the transgressors. (ENOT)

This account of Joseph's rise to a position of trust with the prison warden used much of the same vocabulary as the earlier account of his rise in Potiphar's household. Because this account is shorter, the impression on the reader is more vivid and forceful even than that earlier account.

Several small differences also add to the sense of greater maturity on Joseph's part and greater intimacy between God and Joseph. In the prison, God **showed** Joseph **kindness** (v. 21); that note is absent in the account of Potiphar's household. Whereas Joseph "found favor in [Potiphar's] eyes" (v. 4), God **granted him favor in the eyes of the prison warden** (v. 21). Both Potiphar and the warden placed complete trust in Joseph; as the warden's risk was greater should Joseph breach that trust, we may conclude that the warden's trust in Joseph was deeper. (This is to say nothing of the fact that, in the end, Potiphar believed his unfaithful wife over his faithful steward.)

As the account of Joseph's stewardship over Potiphar's household and estate begins with the notice that he was "a man of success" (v. 2), so the account of his stewardship over the prison ends on that same note; **success** is one of the last words of the chapter (v. 23). God's definition of success is not the financial bottom line, though that line was very good for Potiphar as long as Joseph was his steward. It is not popularity nor the esteem of others; Joseph was successful by God's definition even after Potiphar turned against him and when his fellow prisoner had forgotten him (40:23).

WORDS FROM WESLEY

Genesis 39:21

But the Lord was with Joseph and shewed him mercy. God despiseth not His prisoners, Psalm 69:33. No gates nor bars can shut out His gracious presence from His people. *God gave him favour in the sight of the keeper of the prison*—God can raise up friends for His people even where they little expect them. (ENOT)

God defines success as being faithful in the circumstances in which one finds oneself. Joseph was faithful in his stewardship responsibilities toward Potiphar and the prison warden. He was faithful in maintaining integrity when confronted with sexual temptation. He was faithful to God, who allowed him to know God was with him even when Joseph was imprisoned unjustly. Faithfulness in the circumstances God allows us to experience is a success available to everyone. It requires "only" holding tightly to the hand of the God who is with us, as God was with Joseph.

DISCUSSION

Modern culture tends to measure success by how much money a person has, the size of one's house, the kind of car one drives, or the kind of clothes one wears. Discuss how you measure success. This study focuses on true success.

1. Read Genesis 39:2. What absolute requirement for success do you find in this verse?

2. Why do you agree or disagree that a believer who obeys God is a genuine success regardless of his or her economic or social status?

3. Why do you think God wants to fellowship with you?

4. Why do you agree or disagree that a Christian employee might gain favor in the eyes of a pagan boss?

5. Read Genesis 39:7–12. What help for resisting temptation do you find in Joseph's refusal to succumb to seduction?

6. How does 2 Timothy 2:22 relate to Genesis 39:12 and to your life?

7. How should a believer respond to a false charge?

8. How faithful to God and duty was Joseph in prison?

9. How can you remain faithful to God and therefore experience success when adverse circumstances mount up against you?

PRAYER

Lord, make us the most dependable employees that our supervisors have ever seen, so that You may be glorified through our work.

13

GOD'S PLAN FOR US

Genesis 50:15–26

God has our good in mind.

Has someone hurt you, perhaps lied about you or stolen from you? Laid you off at work or injured you physically? It is easy to hold a grudge and seek revenge, isn't it? But holding a grudge hurts the holder more than the offender. It may not hurt the offender at all.

This study examines Joseph's admirable response to his brothers. Although they had insulted him, thrown him into a pit, sold him into slavery, and then lied to their father about what had become of him, he forgave them when he had the power to imprison or execute them. This study encourages us to forgive those who sin against us.

COMMENTARY

Abraham. Isaac. Jacob. These are the three patriarchs most commonly referenced in the Old Testament. The God of Israel was often referred to as "the God of Abraham, Isaac, and Jacob." But one other hero from the book of Genesis stands out. Of all the characters and stories chronicled in this book, the story of Joseph is perhaps the most memorable. Thirteen chapters are devoted to Joseph's story, far more than to any other single person or event in Genesis. And for good reason.

Joseph's character was impeccable. He endured the scorn and jealousy of his brothers that resulted in him being sold into slavery as a teenager without becoming vengeful or bitter. He was falsely accused, imprisoned, and forgotten. But he never gave up hope. He trusted his God and finally became second in command over all of Egypt, overseeing a food-rationing plan that saved thousands from certain starvation during seven years of severe famine. When circumstances brought his brothers back into his life, Joseph responded with love and forgiveness, moving his entire family to the region of Goshen to be under his care.

His father, Jacob, and his brothers prospered in Goshen, and their families grew. For seventeen years, life was good. And then Jacob died. He was, after all, 147 years old. Joseph and his sons and brothers received blessings from Jacob before his death, and they promised the aging patriarch they would bury him in the land of Canaan in the cave where Abraham and Sarah, Isaac and Rebekah, and his first wife, Leah, were buried. His parting words to Joseph were, "I am about to die, but God will be with you and take you back to the land of your fathers" (Gen. 48:21), a message of hope Joseph later passed on to his own family (50:24–25).

The embalming took forty days, and all of Egypt mourned for Jacob for seventy days before a parade of Egyptian officials and dignitaries accompanied the family on the journey back to Canaan. Jacob's wishes were carried out. And his family returned to the land of Goshen. That's when Joseph's brothers started to worry.

The Blessing of Complete Forgiveness (Gen. 50:15–19, 21)

Although Joseph had shown every sign of having forgiven his brothers, they worried that his kindness would be short-lived with the death of their father: **"What if Joseph holds a grudge against us and pays us back for all the wrongs we did to him?"** (v. 15; see also 27:41, where Esau had planned to kill Jacob as soon as their father, Isaac, died). They had thrown Joseph into a pit and left him for dead. They had sold him as a slave. They had told their father he was killed by a wild animal.

They certainly *deserved* to be treated harshly. If they were in their brother's shoes, *they* would pay themselves back! They had a hard time believing Joseph could really forgive them completely.

WORDS FROM WESLEY

Genesis 50:15

Joseph will peradventure hate us — While their father lived, they thought themselves safe under his shadow; but now he was dead, they feared the worst. A guilty conscience exposeth men to continual frights; those that would be fearless must keep themselves guiltless. (ENOT)

So they sent a message, probably through Benjamin, who had not been a part of the plot to hurt Joseph, stating that Jacob instructed them to tell Joseph **to forgive your brothers the sins and the wrongs they committed in treating you so badly** (50:17). Although it seems more likely that Jacob would have told this to Joseph directly, it is possible that this request was legitimate. Perhaps Jacob wanted the brothers to remember their sin and finally to ask forgiveness from their brother. Their own added comment to the message reveals their contrition: **"Now please forgive the sins of the servants of the God of your father"** (v. 17). They identified themselves as servants of the God of Israel. They were sincere and humble and took responsibility for their previous behavior. The idea that the message was fabricated to coerce Joseph into forgiveness is inconsistent with their behavior at this point. In fact, they **came and threw themselves down before him. "We are your slaves," they said** (v. 18). They had sold him as a slave, but now they were willing to become his slaves. These were men who, even after all these years, still had guilty consciences.

But notice Joseph's response. He **wept** (v. 17) when he read the message, probably moved that they could think he still harbored ill will toward them. Or grieved that they were still bound to the hurts of the past. Joseph immediately set their hearts at ease. **"Don't be afraid. Am I in the place of God?"** (v. 19). **"Don't be afraid. I will provide for you and your children." And he reassured them and spoke kindly to them** (v. 21). Joseph gave to his brothers the blessing of complete forgiveness. He reassured them and spoke gently to them. He promised to provide for them and for their families. His forgiveness was real. It was lasting. The past was behind them. Joseph refused to take the place of God and exact vengeance.

WORDS FROM WESLEY

Genesis 50:17

We are the *servants of the God of thy father*—Not only children of the same Jacob, but worshipers of the same Jehovah. Though we must be ready to forgive all that injure us, yet we must especially take heed of bearing malice towards any that are the servants of the God of our father; those we should always treat with a peculiar tenderness, for we and they have the same master. (ENOT)

Romans 12:19 reminds us, "Do not take revenge, my friends, but leave room for God's wrath, for it is written: 'It is mine to avenge; I will repay,' says the Lord." Joseph lived by a law that hadn't even been written yet (Deut. 32:35). The New Testament reminds us over and over of the importance of forgiveness: If we don't forgive others, God won't forgive us (Matt. 6:14–15); there should be no limit to the number of times we forgive (18:21–22); and no debt owed to us could possibly compare to the debt we owed to God and the magnitude of His forgiveness toward us (18:23–35). The blessing of forgiveness was a gift Joseph gave to his brothers, releasing them from their guilt and fear. But it was also a blessing for Joseph. His forgiveness, which took place long before this point in the story, freed him from enslaving resentment, bitterness, and anger over the cruelty and unjustness of his past.

The Blessing of Complete Faith in God's Providence (Gen. 50:20, 22–26)

Joseph's attitude expressed in verse 20 was the key to his resiliency during desperate times: **"You intended to harm me, but God intended it for good to accomplish what is now being done, the saving of many lives."** He had expressed similar words earlier (see 45:5, 7–8). Joseph believed that "in all things God works for the good of those who love him, who have been called according to his purpose" (Rom. 8:28). He was convinced that God could bring about good in spite of evil. What good had come from Joseph's ill treatment at the hands of his brothers? He had developed character and trust in God. Thousands had been saved during the famine, including his own family. All Israel was relocated to Goshen to be cared for and to develop as a distinct nation until God would lead them back to Canaan. All Joseph could see were the positive results. And so it is whenever we keep our focus on God. We learn to see His hand at work in the midst of our struggles. Paul was also a master at this. He wrote, "Therefore we do not lose heart. Though outwardly we are wasting away, yet inwardly we are being renewed day by day. For our light and momentary troubles are achieving for us an eternal glory that far outweighs them all. So we fix our eyes not on what is seen, but on what is unseen. For what is seen is temporary, but what is unseen is eternal" (2 Cor. 4:16–18).

We must be careful not to condone evil on the basis that if good comes from it, the evil must have been God's will. Paul wrote, "What shall we say, then? Shall we go on sinning so that grace may increase? By no means!" (Rom. 6:1–2). Instead, we simply recognize that God is in control. He can make good come from bad. When people intend harm, God can bring blessing. When evil thinks it has scored a victory, God has the last word. Those who trust in Him are never left helpless and hopeless.

WORDS FROM WESLEY

Genesis 50:21

Fear not, I will nourish you—See what an excellent spirit Joseph was of, and learn of him to render good for evil. He did not tell them they were upon their good behaviour, and he would be kind to them if he saw they carried themselves well: no, he would not thus hold them in suspence, nor seem jealous of them, though they had been suspicious of him. He comforted them, and, to banish all their fears, he spake kindly to them. Those we love and forgive we must not only do well for, but speak kindly to. (ENOT)

Joseph reminded his **brothers** (Gen. 50:24, probably a reference to the larger family, since by this time his brothers may have already died) before his death, **"God will surely come to your aid and take you up out of this land. . . . God will surely come to your aid"** (vv. 24–25). Joseph had an unshakable confidence in God's providence. He knew God would rescue them. He knew God would fulfill His promise to Abraham, Isaac, and Jacob to give Israel the land of Canaan. He wanted to pass this faith—this hope—along to the next generations. He made them **swear an oath** (v. 25) to bury his bones in Canaan when that time came, so sure was he that the time *would* come. Their promise would make them determined to hold fast to the hope of returning to Canaan.

Joseph's faith in God's promises was a blessing to others. He was able to encourage his family and instill faith in them because of his own confidence in God. But his faith was a blessing to him, too. It allowed him to be forward-looking instead of backward-looking. Joseph didn't have time to dwell on the past when he was looking forward to the future God had promised. He didn't have to live with "what-ifs" and the fear of what might lie ahead. Like the apostle Paul, Joseph learned to be content in every situation (Phil. 4:11), because he knew his God was in control.

Verses 22 and 26 tell us that Joseph lived to be 110 years old, considered by the Egyptians to be the perfect lifespan—an indication that one had received divine blessing. And Joseph had. God enabled him to see **the third generation of Ephraim's children. Also the children of Makir son of Manasseh were placed at birth on Joseph's knees** (v. 23). God allowed Joseph to see his great-great-grandchildren, even adopting Makir's children as his own. Joseph's life wasn't always easy, but the end result was proof of God's blessing upon his life.

WORDS FROM WESLEY
Genesis 50:25

And ye shall carry up my bones from hence—Herein he had an eye to the promise, Gen. 15:13, 14 and in God's name assures them of the performance of it. In Egypt they buried their great men very honourably, and with abundance of pomp; but Joseph prefers a plain burial in Canaan, and that deferred almost two hundred years, before a magnificent one in Egypt. Thus Joseph by faith in the doctrine of the resurrection, and the promise of Canaan, gave commandment concerning his bones, Heb. 11:22. He dies in Egypt; but lays his bones at stake, that God will surely visit Israel, and bring them to Canaan. (ENOT)

Joseph was **embalmed** (a forty-day process for which the Egyptians were famous) and **placed in a coffin in Egypt** (v. 26). His bones wouldn't reach the Promised Land for another 360 years. Genesis begins in a garden, but ends in a graveyard. It seems like a bleak ending to a story that began with so much promise. But God wasn't finished with His plan for His people.

Joseph has often been viewed by theologians throughout history as a "type" of Christ. His character and life were an illustration of what the Messiah would be like. Jesus, who would be betrayed by His own "brothers," would also say on the cross, "Father, forgive them, for they do not know what they are doing" (Luke 23:34). He left His disciples with the promise that He would come back (John 14; Matt. 24). Jesus exemplified forgiveness and faith. It is fair, then, to say that Joseph was Christlike. He is a powerful example for us that we can live like Jesus. We can experience the blessings that come from knowing His forgiveness and forgiving others. We can experience the blessing of complete confidence in God's providence in our lives. And we can pass that hope, that confident assurance, on to future generations.

DISCUSSION

Discuss reactions to the statement "I can forgive, but I can't forget." Discuss if forgiveness is complete if we harbor the memory of the offense.

1. What sins had Joseph's brothers committed against him? Which one do you think was most heinous? Why?

2. What evidence do you see in the brothers' visit to Joseph that his early dream was now fulfilled? Are you willing to wait a long time for God to fulfill His will? Why or why not?

3. Why do you agree or disagree that holding a grudge hurts the person who holds the grudge more than it hurts the objects of the grudge?

4. Is it hard to trust God to right whatever wrongs have been committed against you? Why or why not?

5. How can you "forget" (put behind you) an offense even though you can remember it if you choose to?

6. If a member of your congregation mars the church's testimony by sinning, should the church simply overlook the sin? If not, what action might be appropriate?

7. Why do you agree or disagree that sin is often condoned? What accountability might a church put in place to discourage sinning?

8. How do events in Joseph's life remind you of similar events in Jesus' life?

PRAYER

Lord, keep us ever ready to show mercy to those who request it. Let us never forget how merciful You have been to us.

WORDS FROM WESLEY WORKS CITED

ENOT: Wesley, J. (1765). *Explanatory Notes upon the Old Testament* (Vol. 1–3). Bristol: William Pine.

PW: *The Poetical Works of John and Charles Wesley.* Edited by D. D. G. Osborn. 13 vols. London: Wesleyan-Methodist Conference Office, 1868.

WJW: *The Works of John Wesley.* Third Edition, Complete and Unabridged. 14 vols. London: Wesleyan Methodist Book Room, 1872.

OTHER BOOKS IN THE
WESLEY BIBLE STUDIES SERIES

Now Available in the Wesley Bible Studies Series

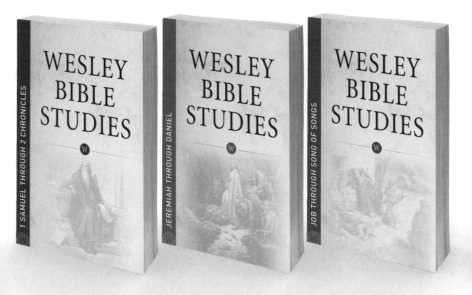

Each book in the Wesley Bible Studies series provides a thoughtful and powerful survey of key Scriptures in one or more biblical books. They combine accessible commentary from contemporary teachers, with relevantly highlighted direct quotes from the complete writings and life experiences of John Wesley, along with the poetry and hymns of his brother Charles. For each study, creative and engaging questions foster deeper fellowship and growth.

1 Samuel through 2 Chronicles
978-0-89827-866-8
978-0-89827-867-5 (e-book)

Jeremiah through Daniel
978-0-89827-868-2
978-0-89827-869-9 (e-book)

Job through Song of Songs
978-0-89827-836-1
978-0-89827-837-8 (e-book)

1.800.493.7539 wphstore.com